Hudson 1/2/19

G.I. JOE® Combat Heroes

WE ARE G.I. JOE!

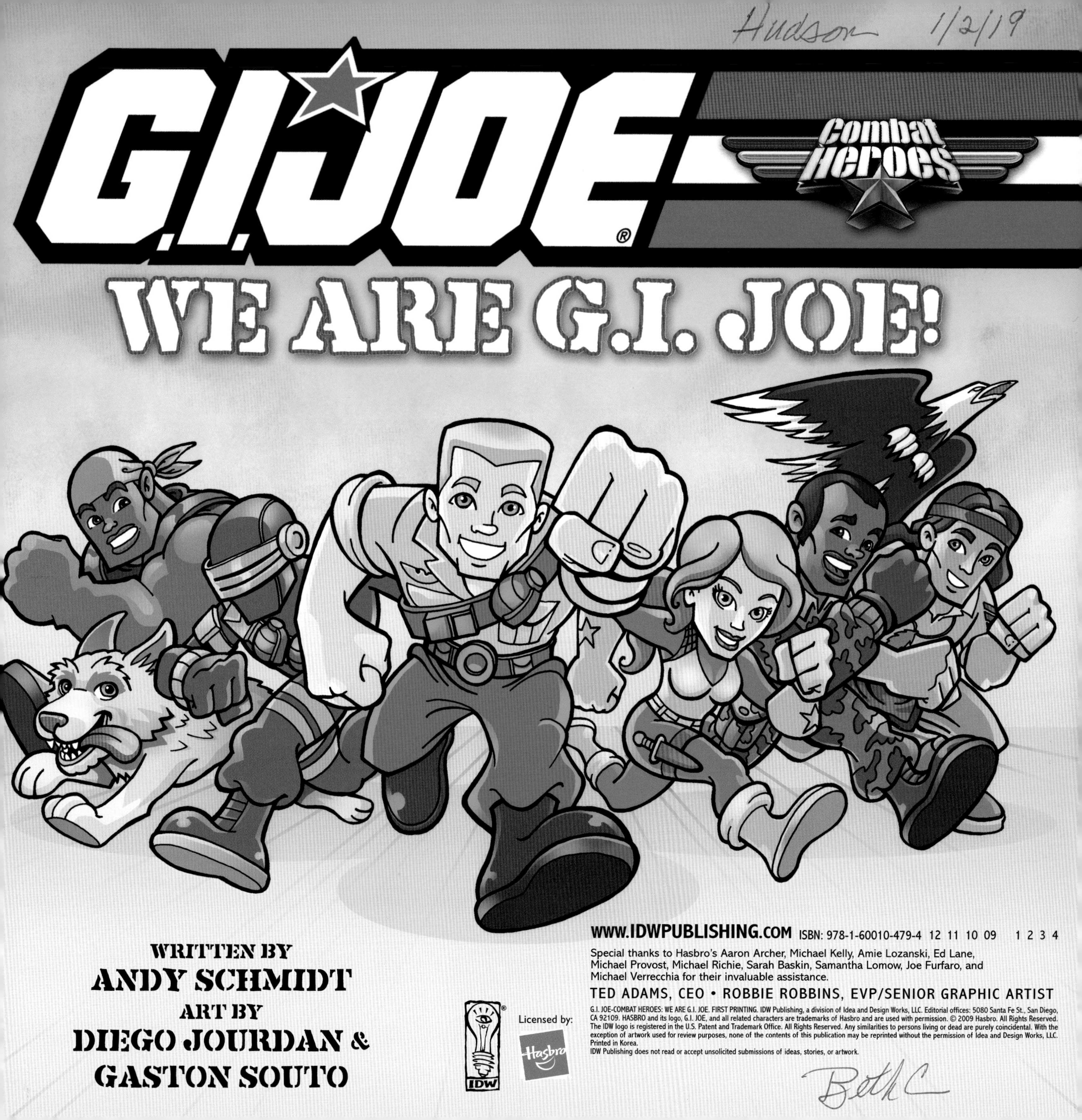

WRITTEN BY
ANDY SCHMIDT
ART BY
DIEGO JOURDAN & GASTON SOUTO

WWW.IDWPUBLISHING.COM ISBN: 978-1-60010-479-4 12 11 10 09 1 2 3 4

Special thanks to Hasbro's Aaron Archer, Michael Kelly, Amie Lozanski, Ed Lane, Michael Provost, Michael Richie, Sarah Baskin, Samantha Lomow, Joe Furfaro, and Michael Verrecchia for their invaluable assistance.

TED ADAMS, CEO • ROBBIE ROBBINS, EVP/SENIOR GRAPHIC ARTIST

Licensed by: Hasbro

Beth C

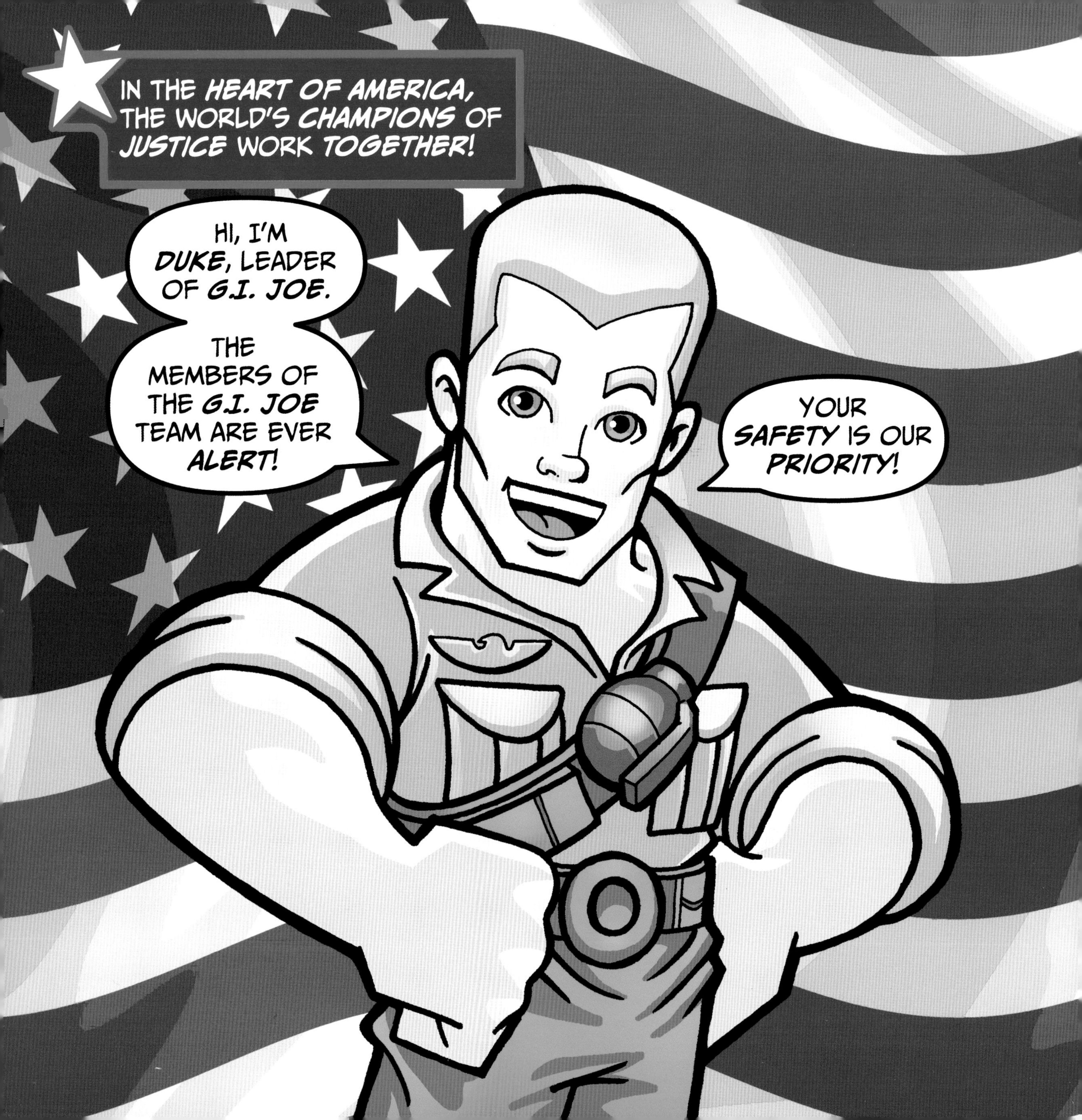
IN THE HEART OF AMERICA, THE WORLD'S CHAMPIONS OF JUSTICE WORK TOGETHER!
HI, I'M DUKE, LEADER OF G.I. JOE.
THE MEMBERS OF THE G.I. JOE TEAM ARE EVER ALERT!
YOUR SAFETY IS OUR PRIORITY!

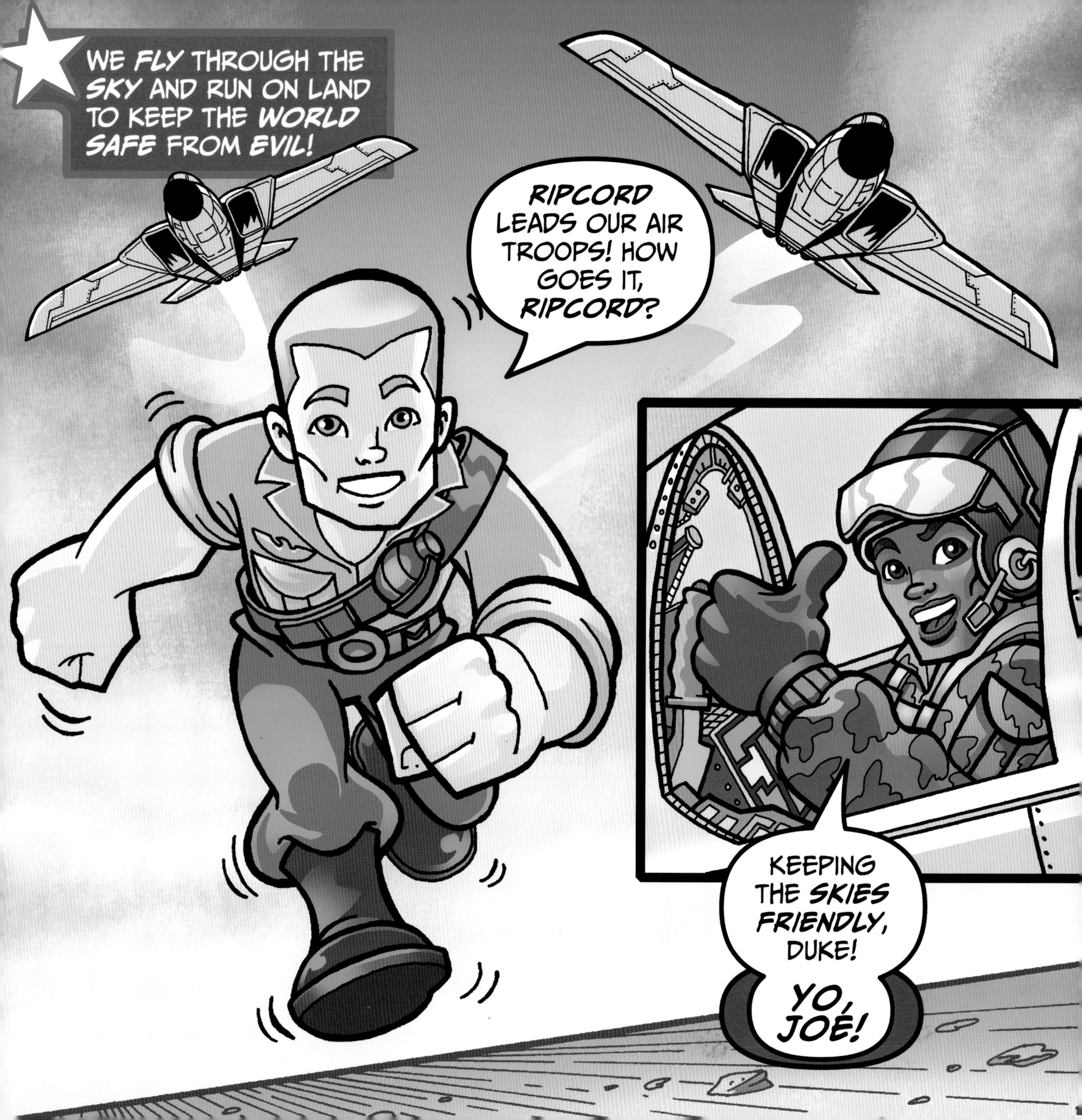
WE FLY THROUGH THE SKY AND RUN ON LAND TO KEEP THE WORLD SAFE FROM EVIL!
RIPCORD LEADS OUR AIR TROOPS! HOW GOES IT, RIPCORD?
KEEPING THE SKIES FRIENDLY, DUKE!
YO, JOE!

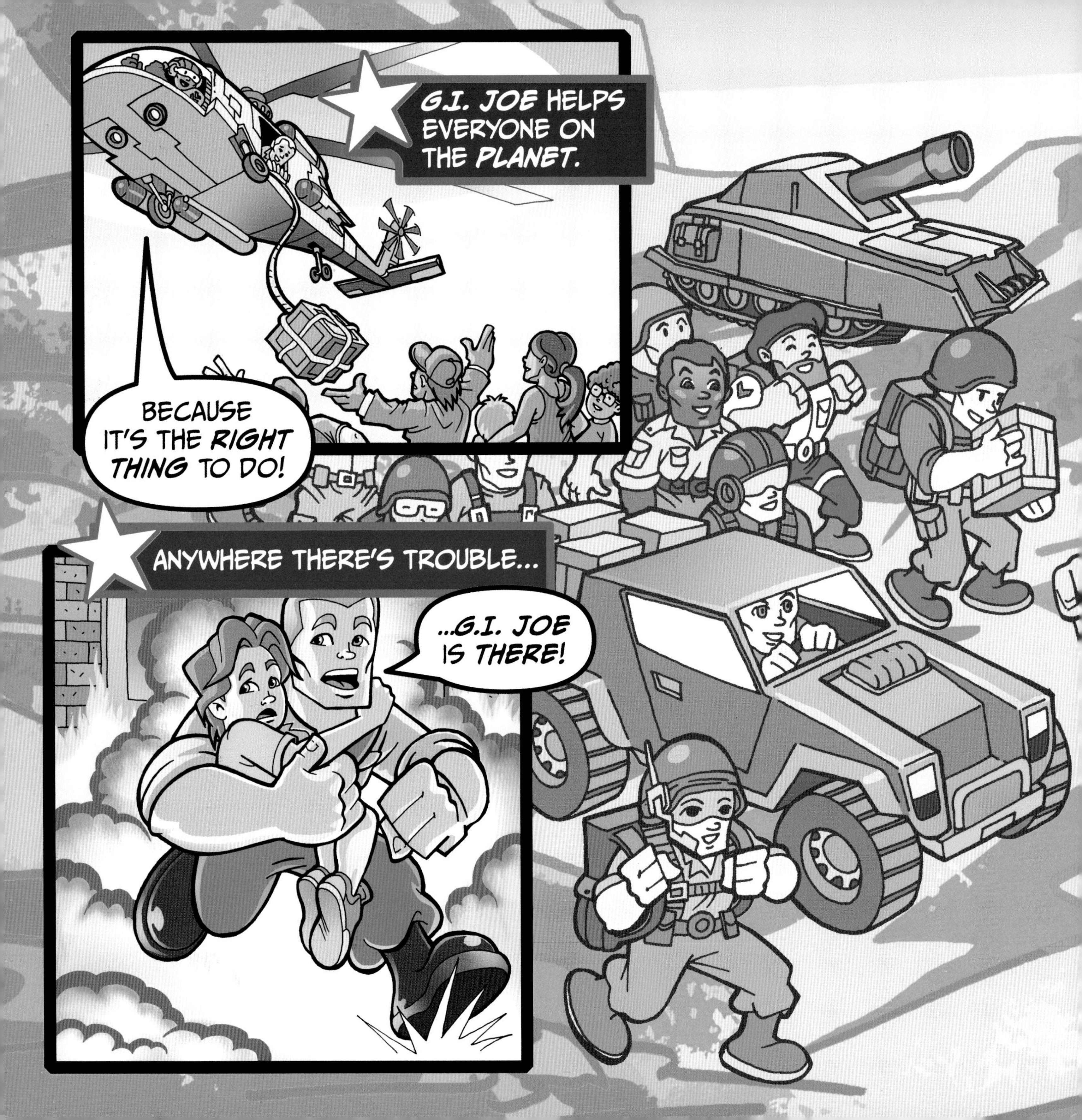
G.I. JOE HELPS EVERYONE ON THE PLANET.
BECAUSE IT'S THE RIGHT THING TO DO!
ANYWHERE THERE'S TROUBLE...
...G.I. JOE IS THERE!

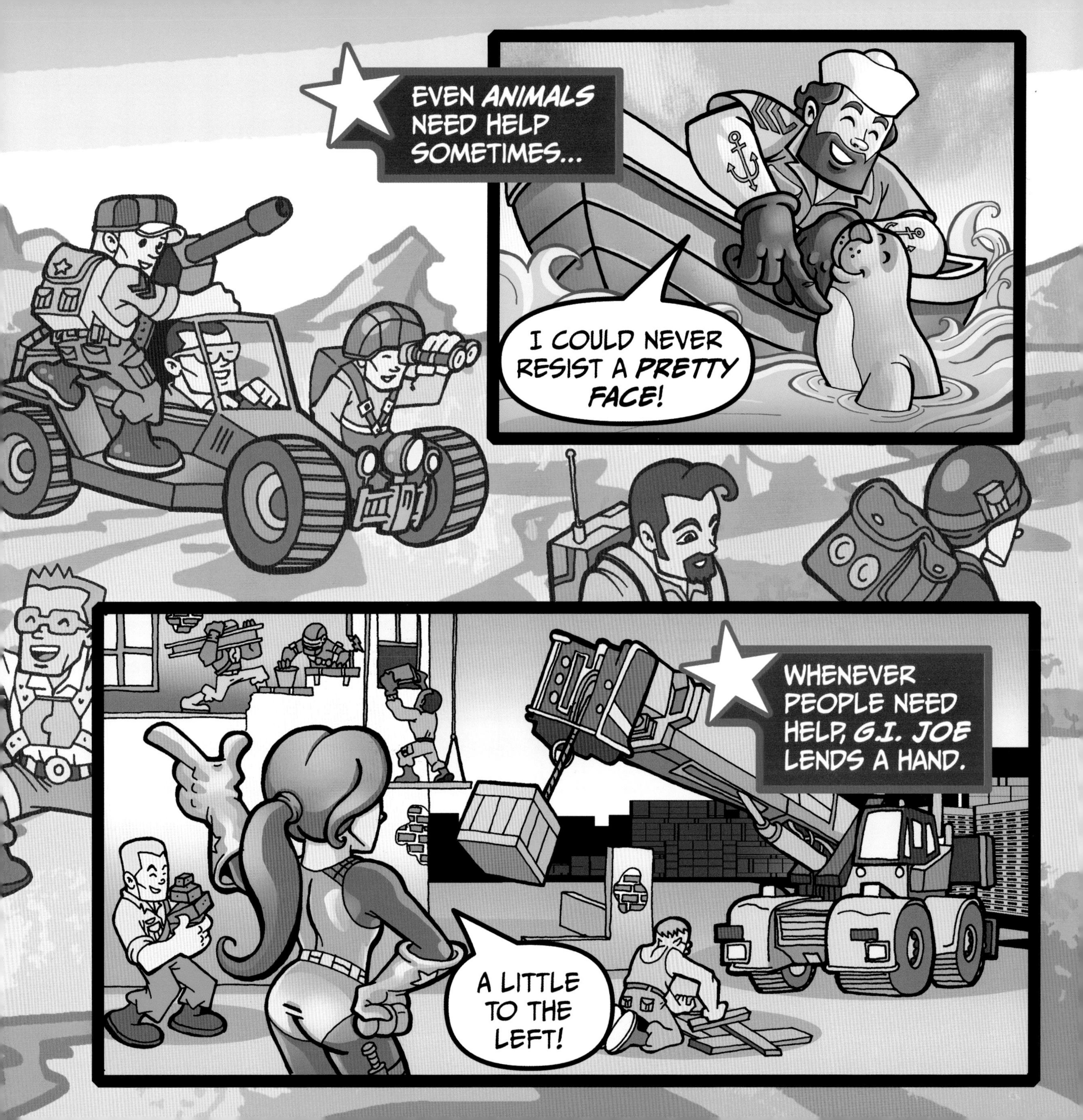
EVEN ANIMALS NEED HELP SOMETIMES...
I COULD NEVER RESIST A PRETTY FACE!
WHENEVER PEOPLE NEED HELP, G.I. JOE LENDS A HAND.
A LITTLE TO THE LEFT!

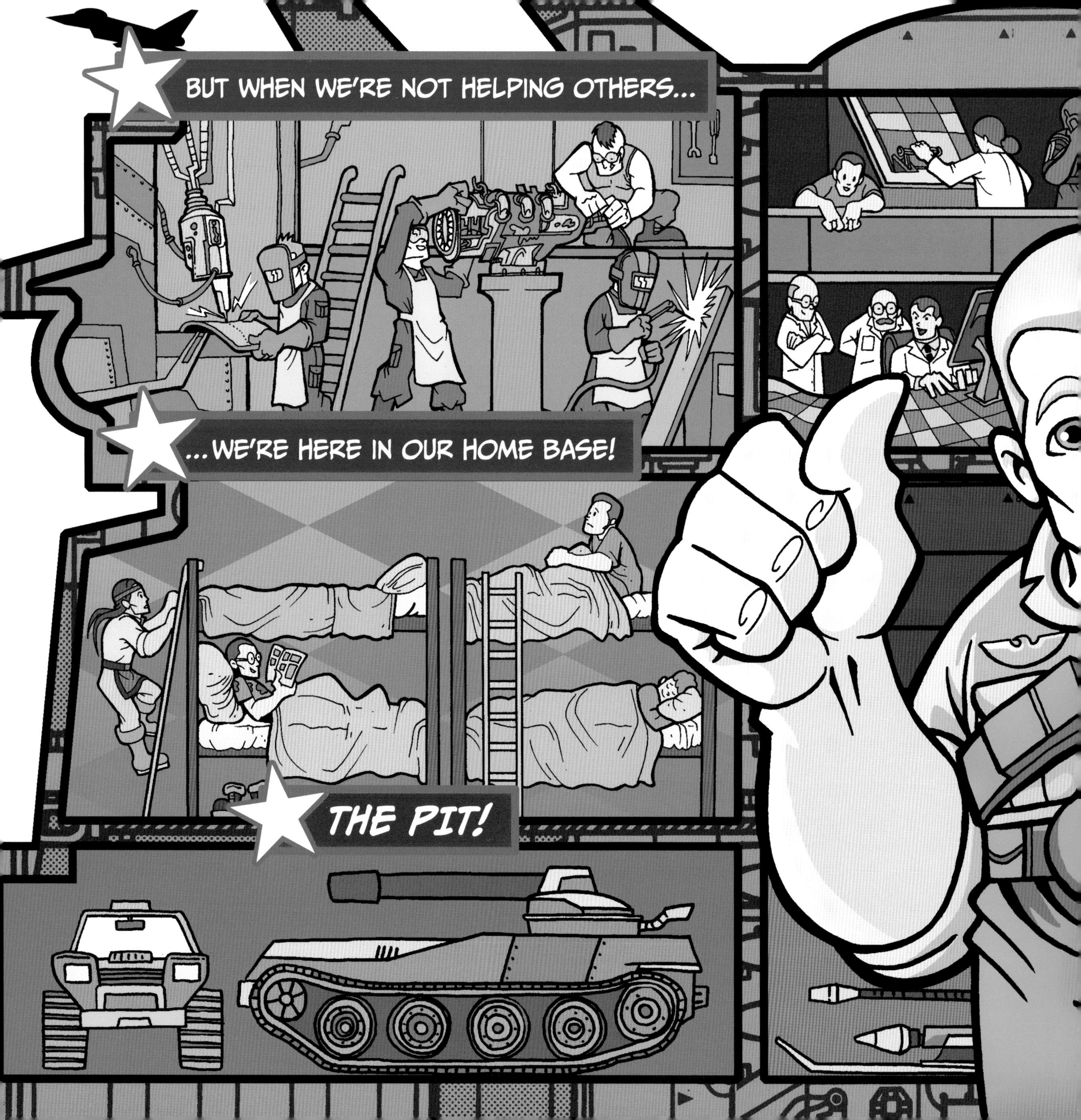
BUT WHEN WE'RE NOT HELPING OTHERS...
...WE'RE HERE IN OUR HOME BASE!
THE PIT!

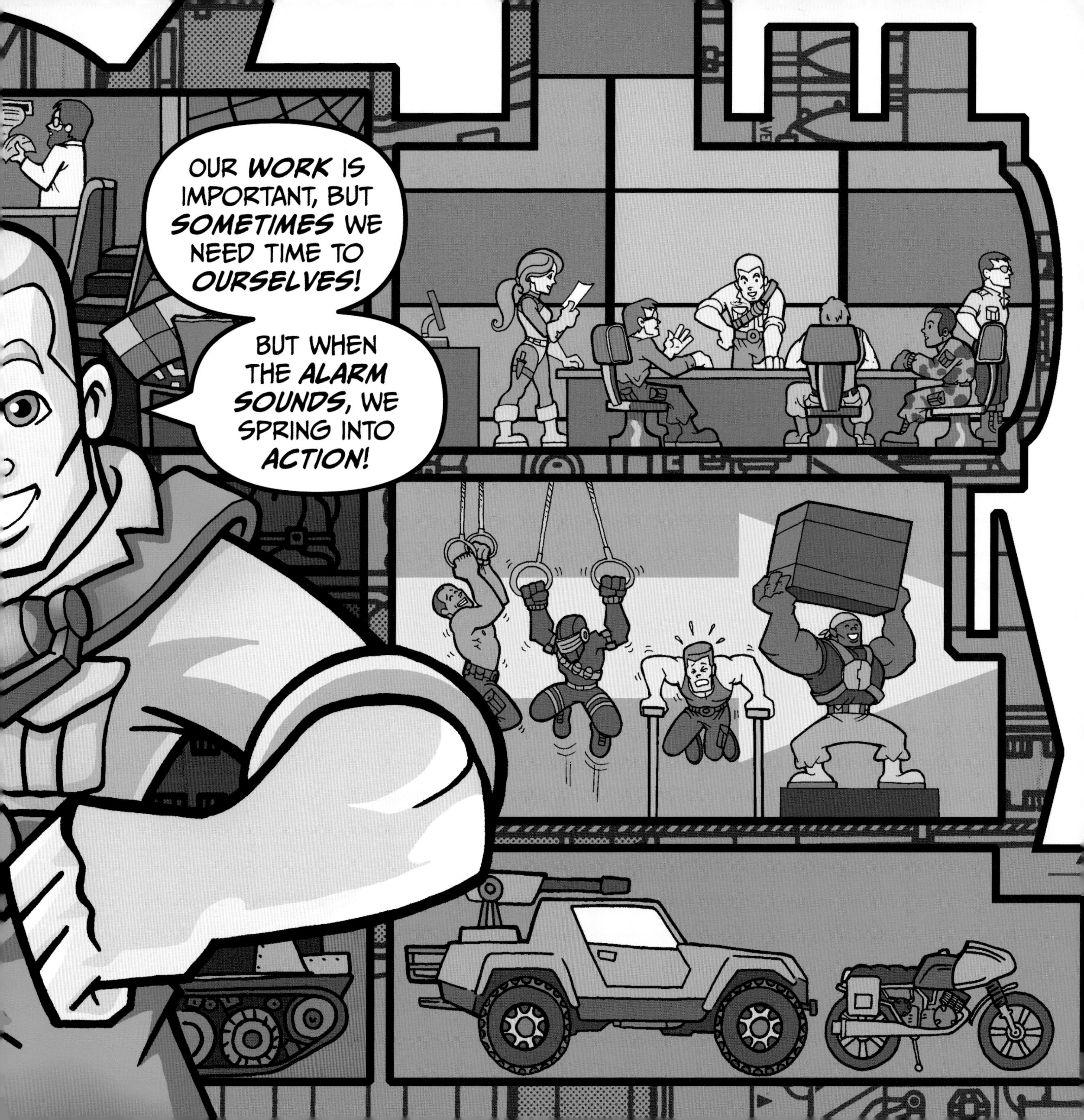
OUR WORK IS IMPORTANT, BUT SOMETIMES WE NEED TIME TO OURSELVES!
BUT WHEN THE ALARM SOUNDS, WE SPRING INTO ACTION!

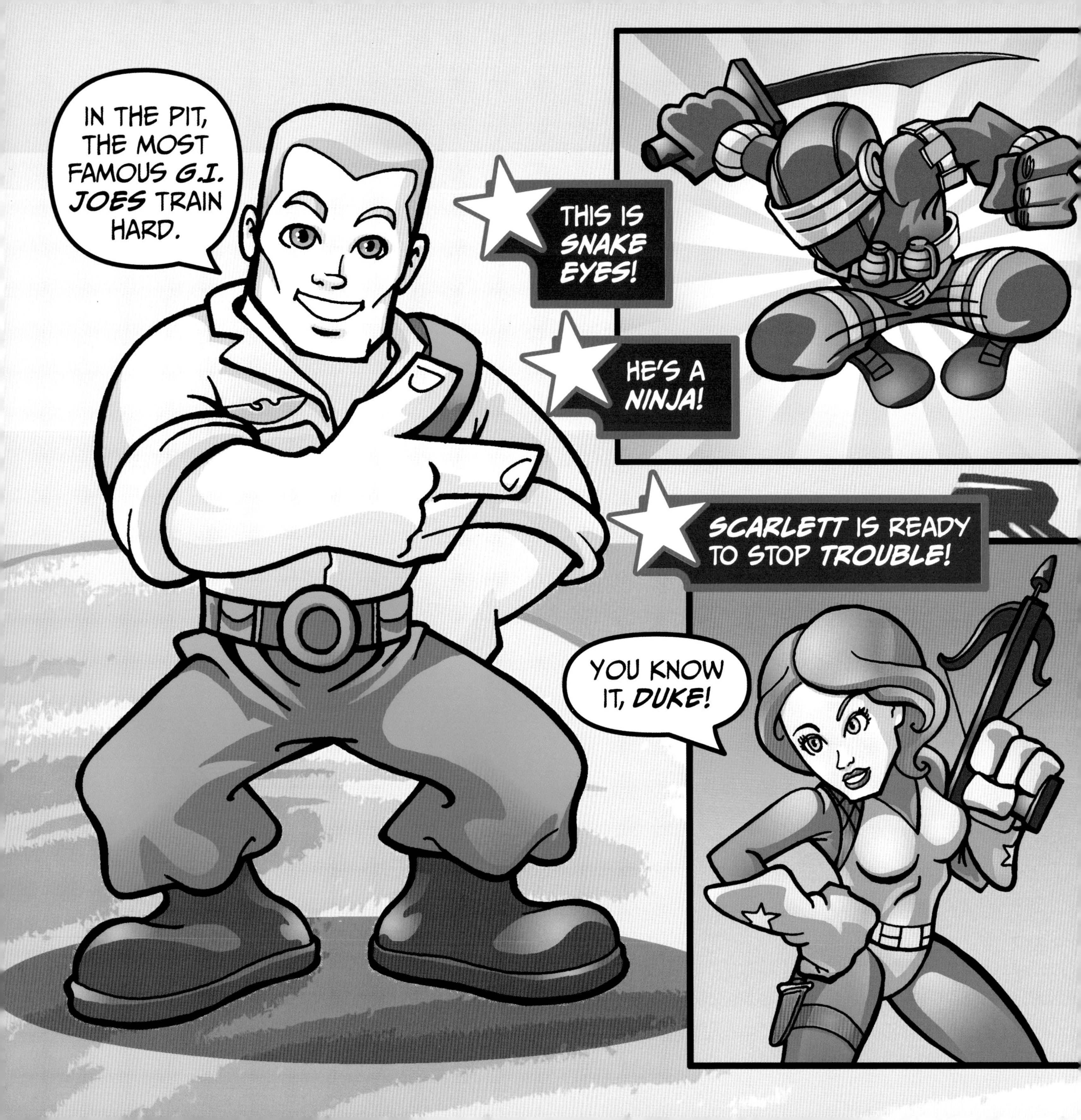

IN THE PIT, THE MOST FAMOUS G.I. JOES TRAIN HARD.
THIS IS SNAKE EYES!
HE'S A NINJA!
SCARLETT IS READY TO STOP TROUBLE!
YOU KNOW IT, DUKE!

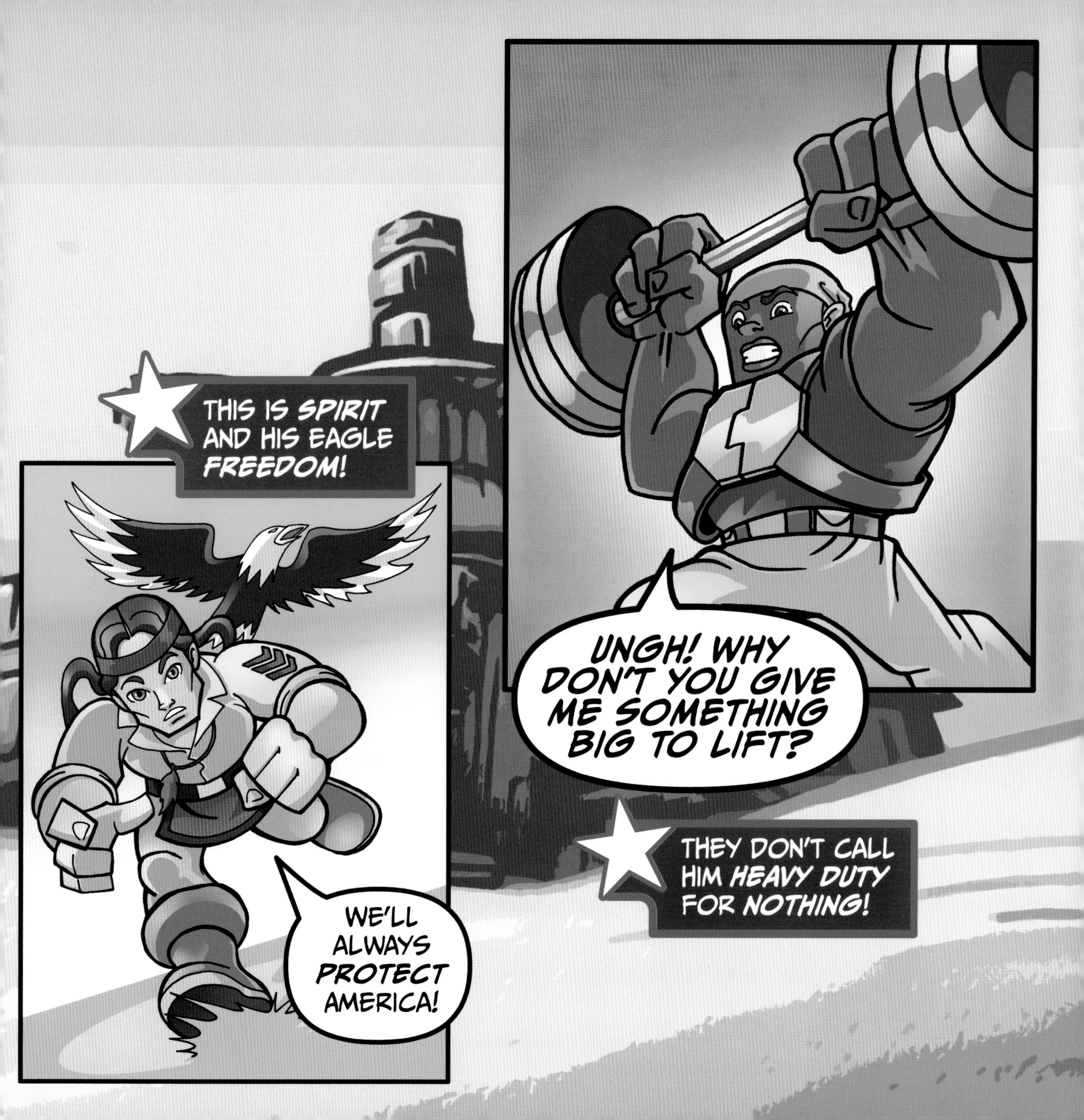
THIS IS SPIRIT AND HIS EAGLE FREEDOM!
WE'LL ALWAYS PROTECT AMERICA!
UNGH! WHY DON'T YOU GIVE ME SOMETHING BIG TO LIFT?
THEY DON'T CALL HIM HEAVY DUTY FOR NOTHING!

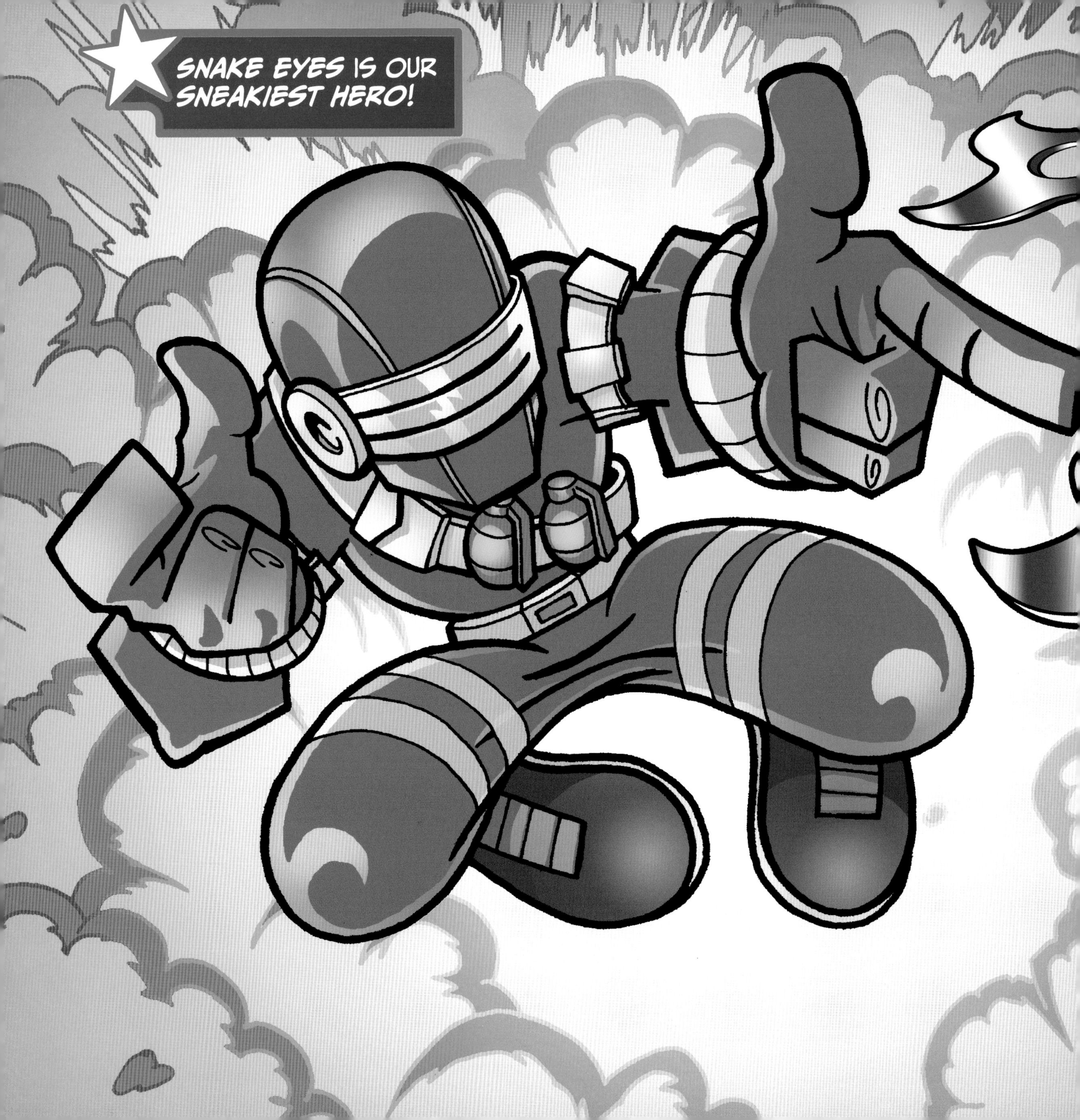
SNAKE EYES IS OUR SNEAKIEST HERO!

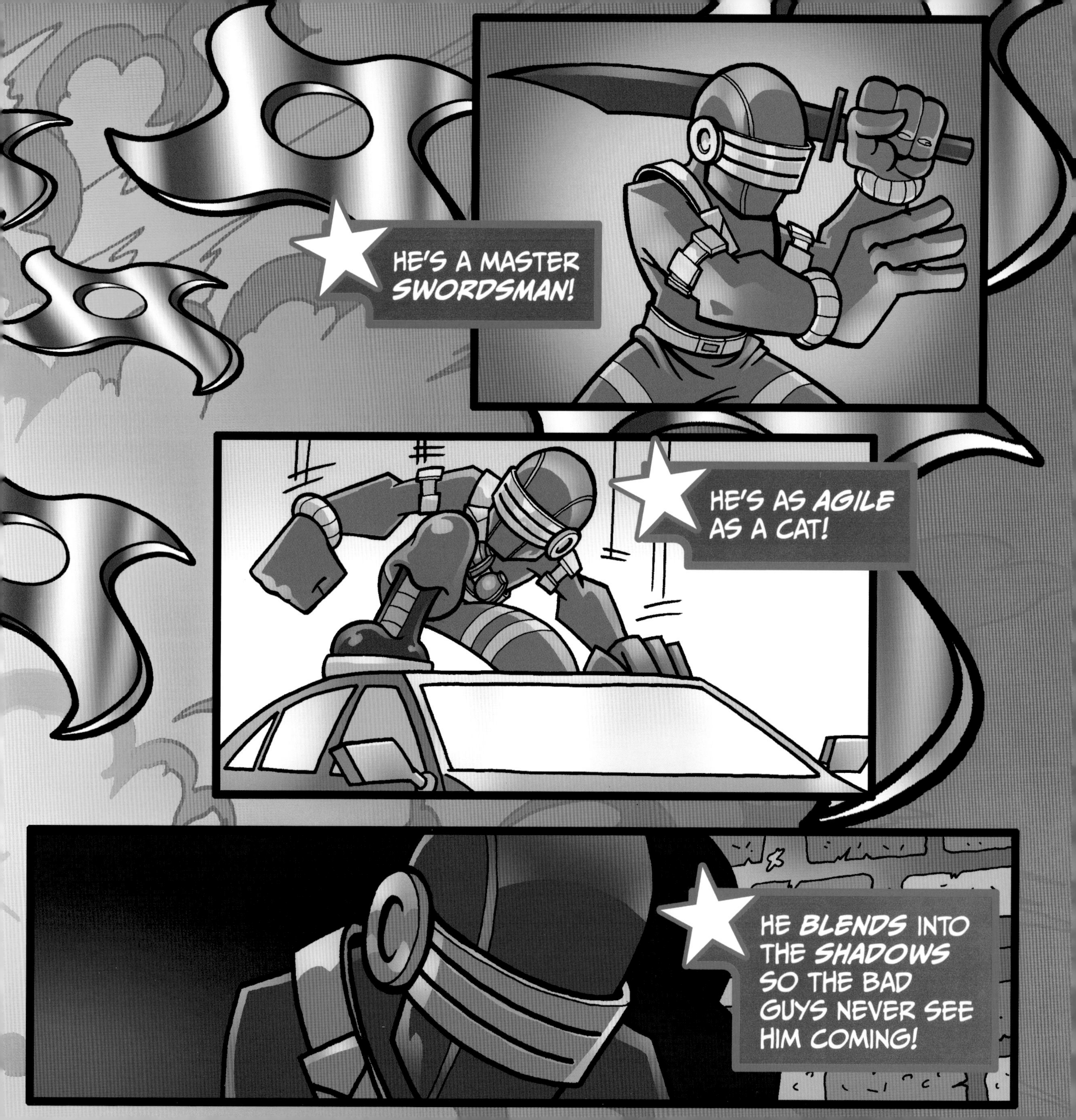
HE'S A MASTER SWORDSMAN!
HE'S AS AGILE AS A CAT!
HE BLENDS INTO THE SHADOWS SO THE BAD GUYS NEVER SEE HIM COMING!

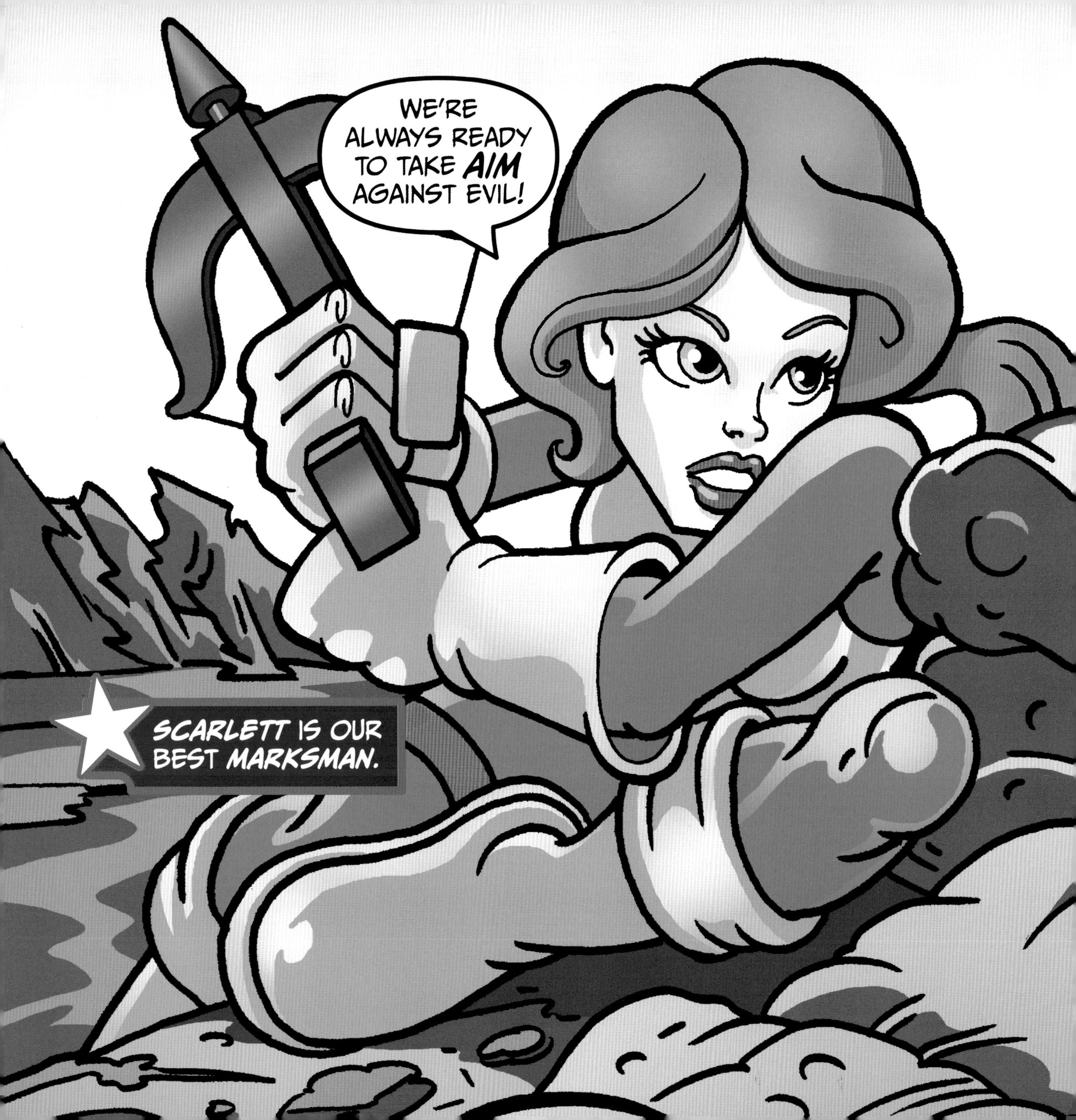
WE'RE ALWAYS READY TO TAKE AIM AGAINST EVIL!
SCARLETT IS OUR BEST MARKSMAN.

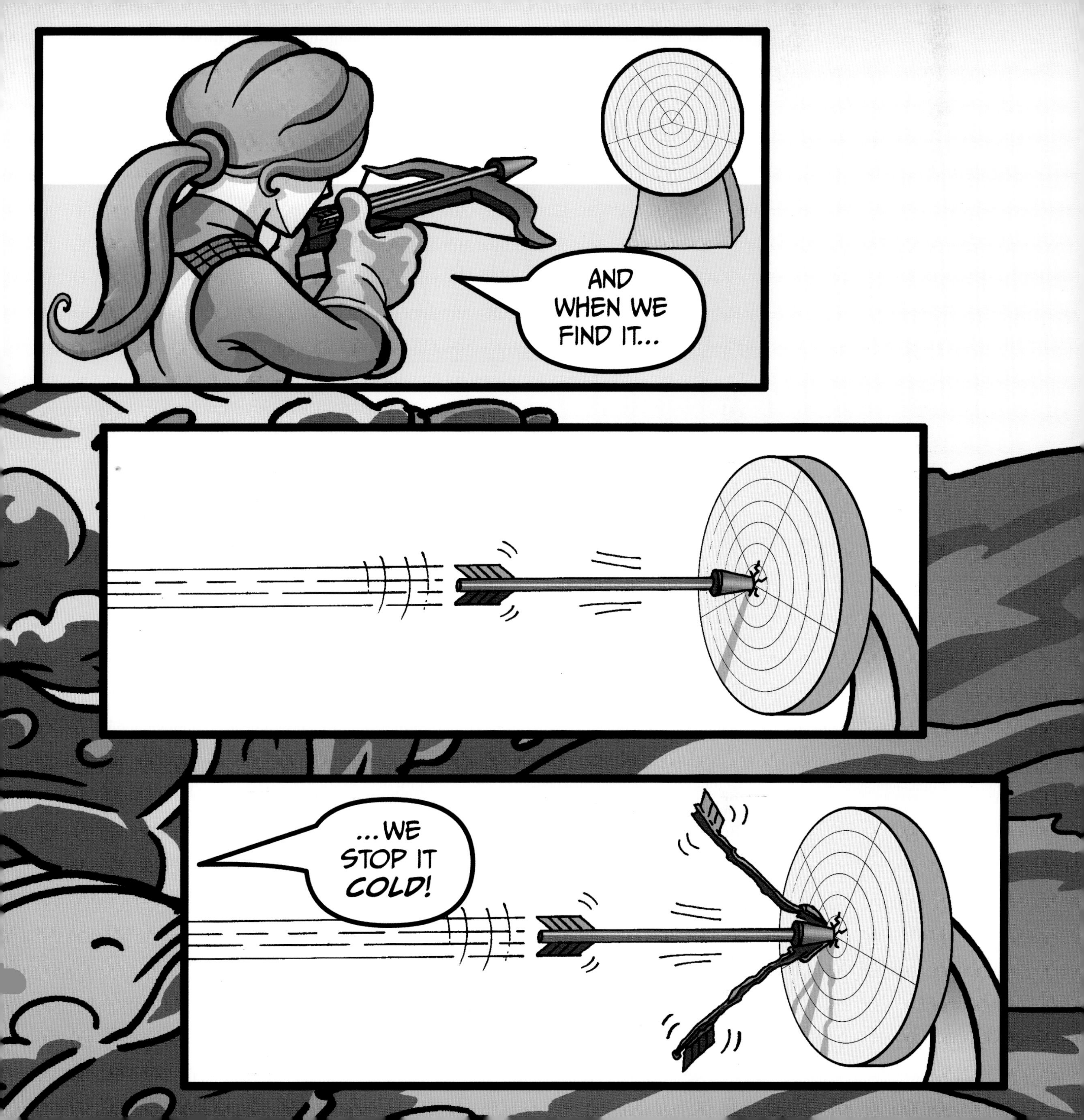
AND WHEN WE FIND IT...
...WE STOP IT COLD!

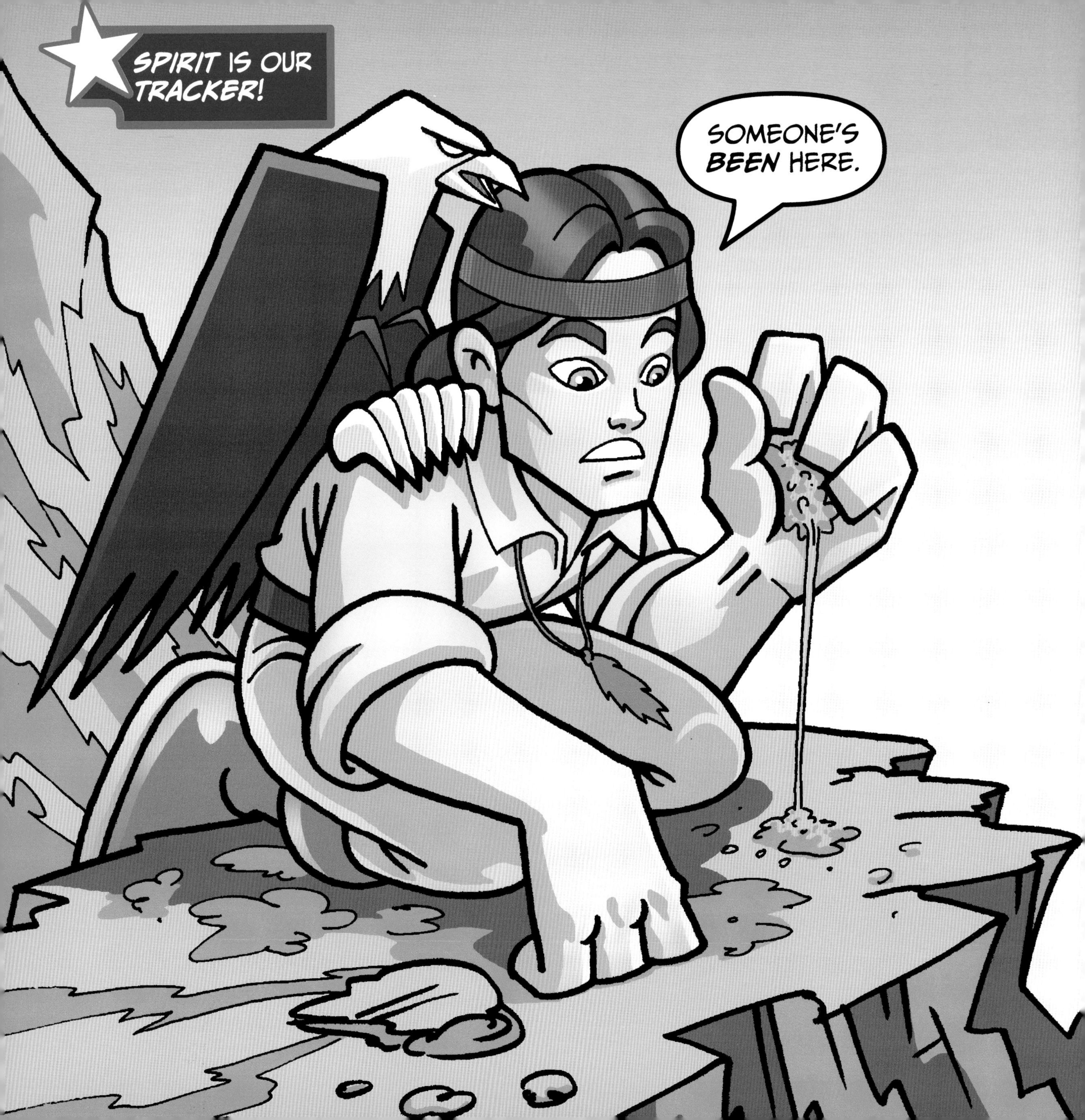
SPIRIT IS OUR TRACKER!
SOMEONE'S BEEN HERE.

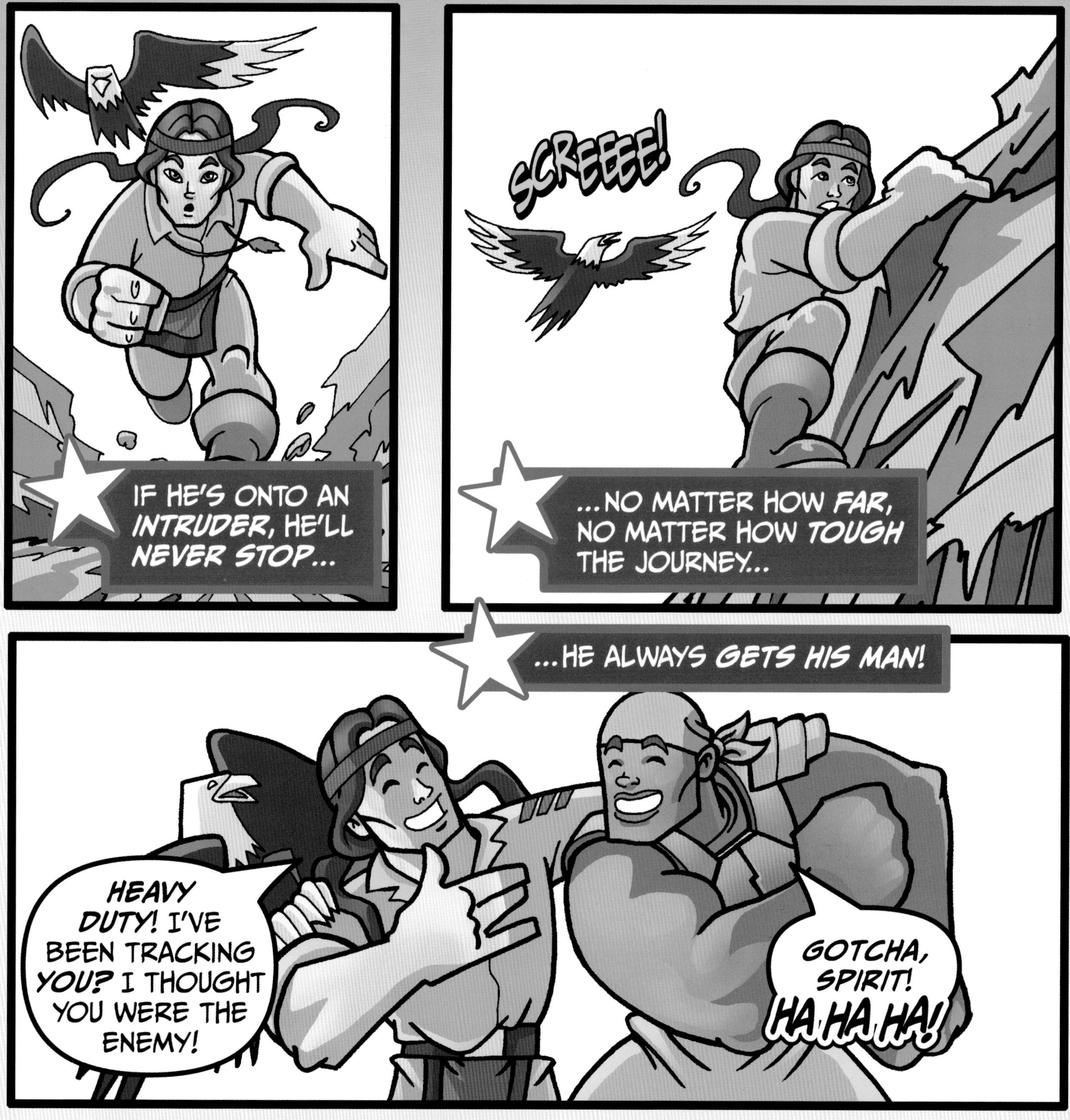
IF HE'S ONTO AN INTRUDER, HE'LL NEVER STOP...
SCREEEEE!
...NO MATTER HOW FAR, NO MATTER HOW TOUGH THE JOURNEY...
...HE ALWAYS GETS HIS MAN!
HEAVY DUTY! I'VE BEEN TRACKING YOU? I THOUGHT YOU WERE THE ENEMY!
GOTCHA, SPIRIT! HA HA HA!

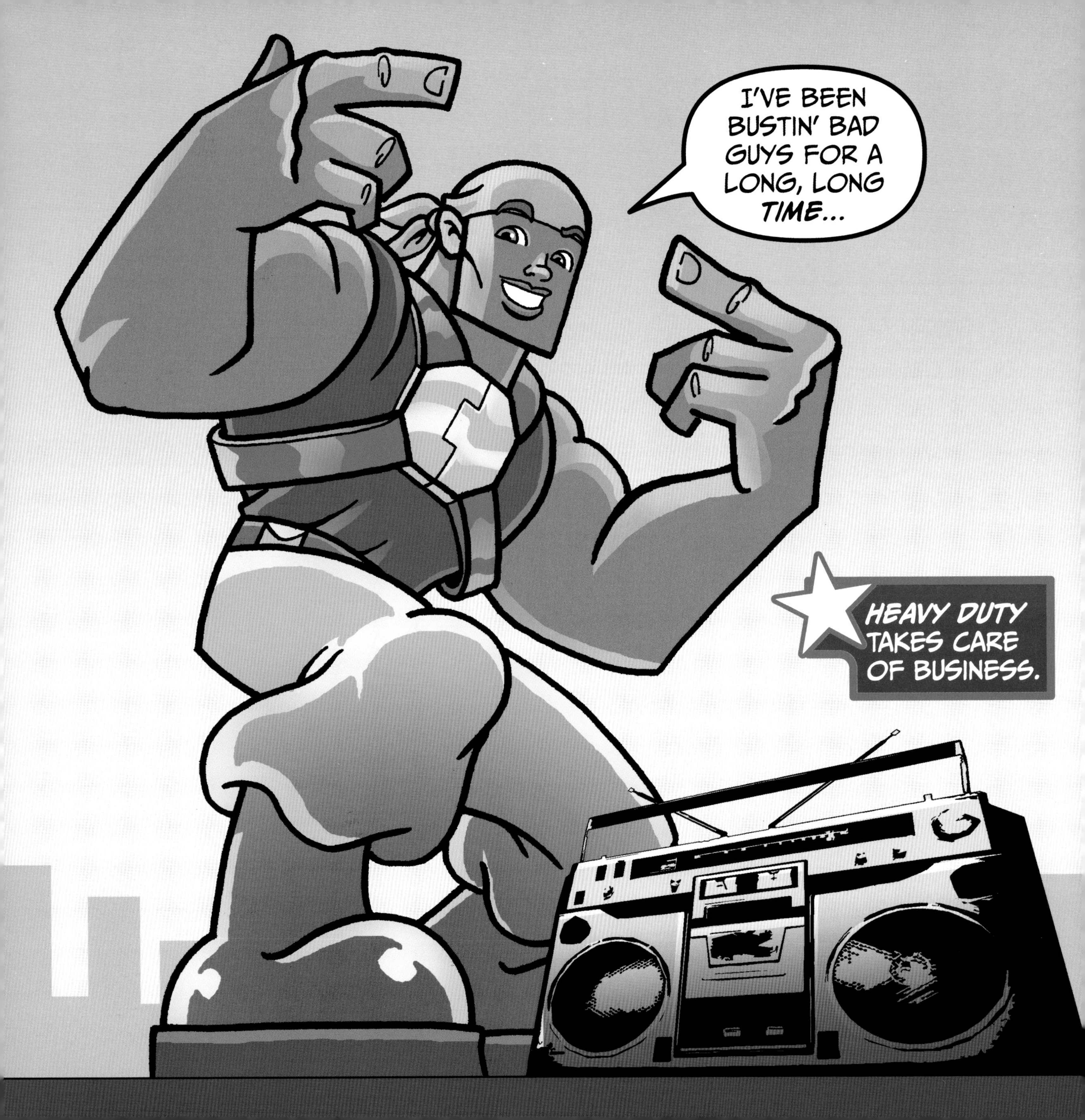
I'VE BEEN BUSTIN' BAD GUYS FOR A LONG, LONG *TIME*...
HEAVY DUTY TAKES CARE OF BUSINESS.

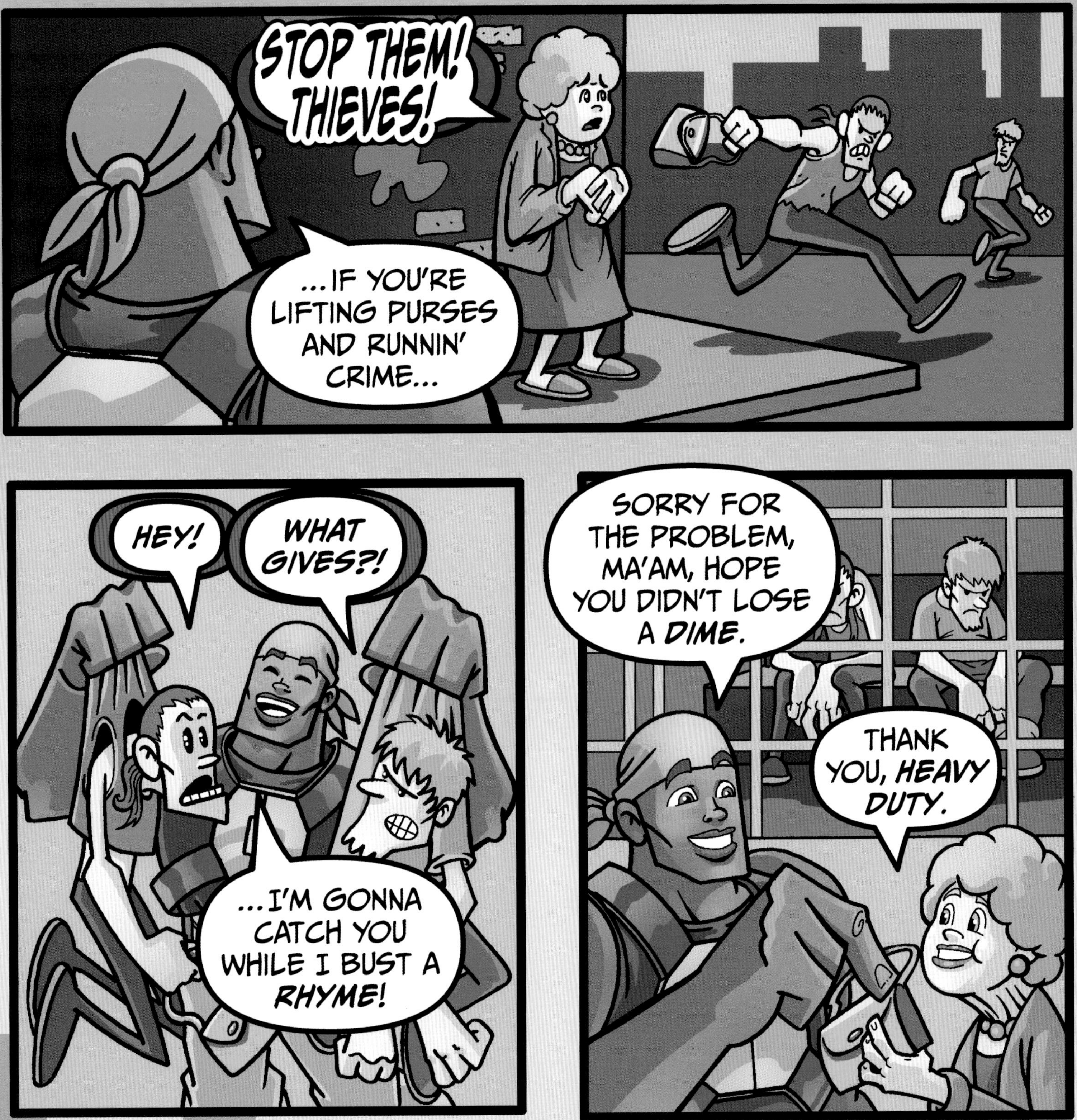
STOP THEM! THIEVES!
...IF YOU'RE LIFTING PURSES AND RUNNIN' CRIME...
HEY!
WHAT GIVES?!
...I'M GONNA CATCH YOU WHILE I BUST A *RHYME!*
SORRY FOR THE PROBLEM, MA'AM, HOPE YOU DIDN'T LOSE A *DIME.*
THANK YOU, *HEAVY DUTY.*

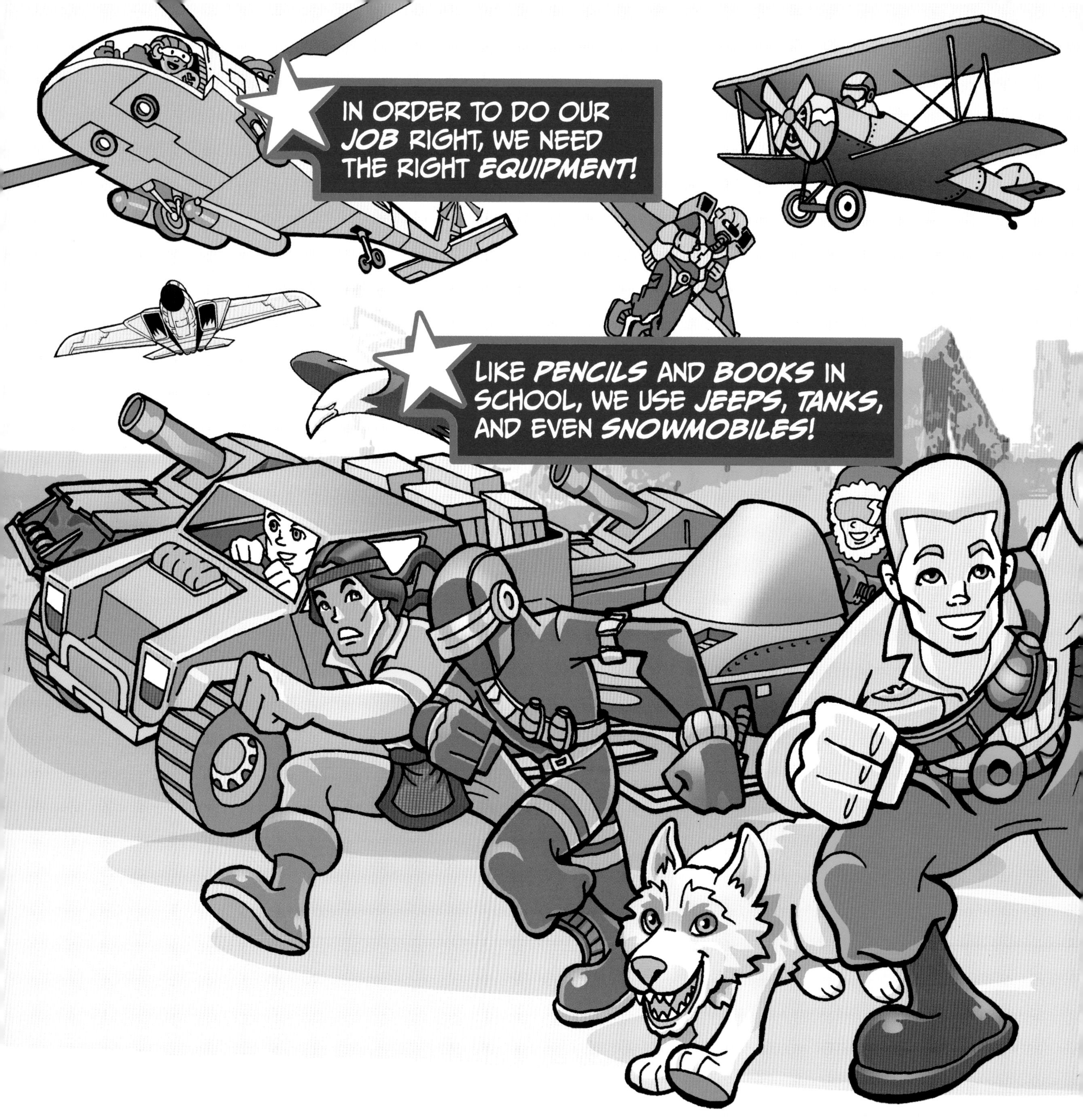
IN ORDER TO DO OUR JOB RIGHT, WE NEED THE RIGHT EQUIPMENT!
LIKE PENCILS AND BOOKS IN SCHOOL, WE USE JEEPS, TANKS, AND EVEN SNOWMOBILES!

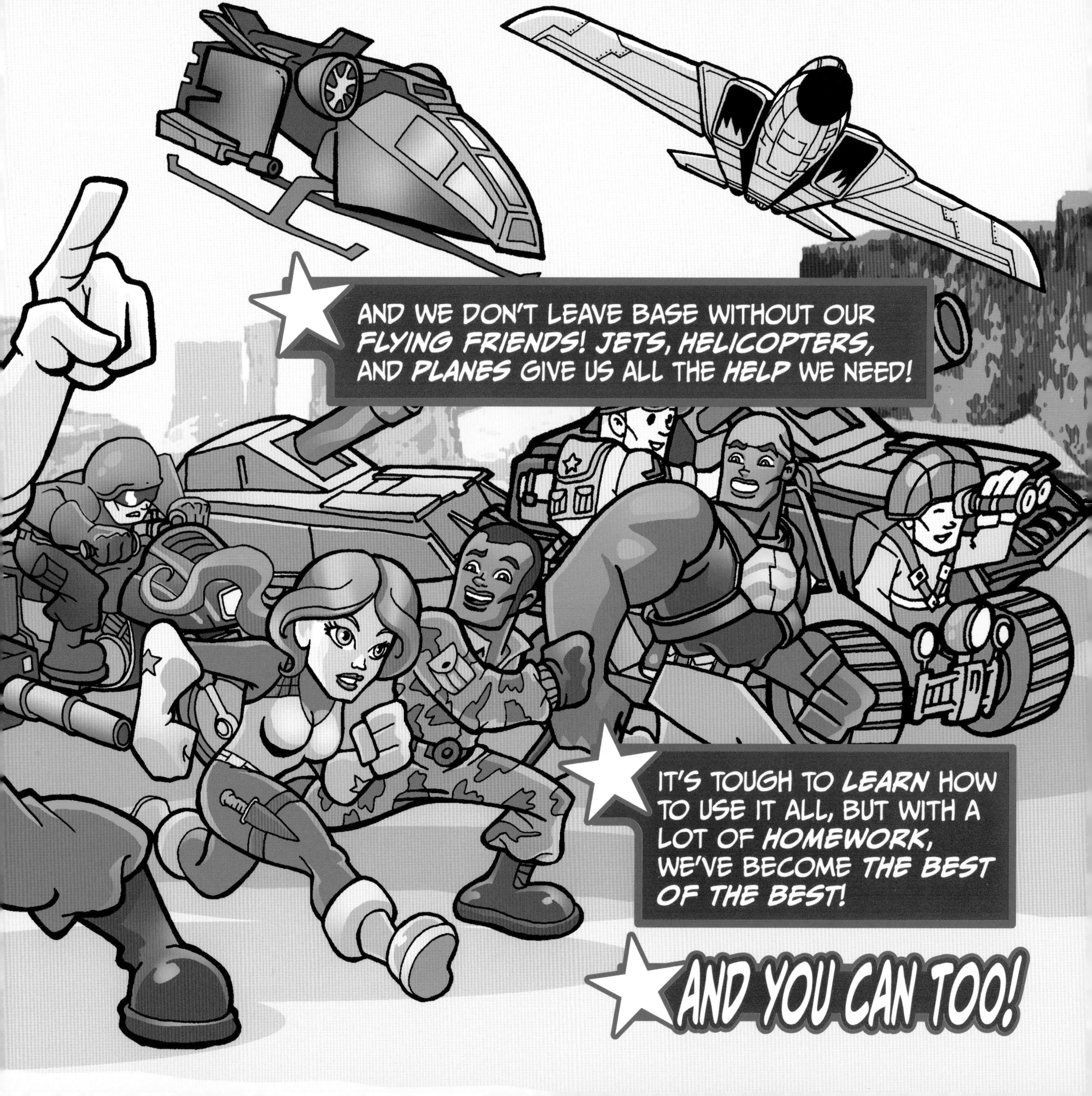
AND WE DON'T LEAVE BASE WITHOUT OUR FLYING FRIENDS! JETS, HELICOPTERS, AND PLANES GIVE US ALL THE HELP WE NEED!
IT'S TOUGH TO LEARN HOW TO USE IT ALL, BUT WITH A LOT OF HOMEWORK, WE'VE BECOME THE BEST OF THE BEST!
AND YOU CAN TOO!

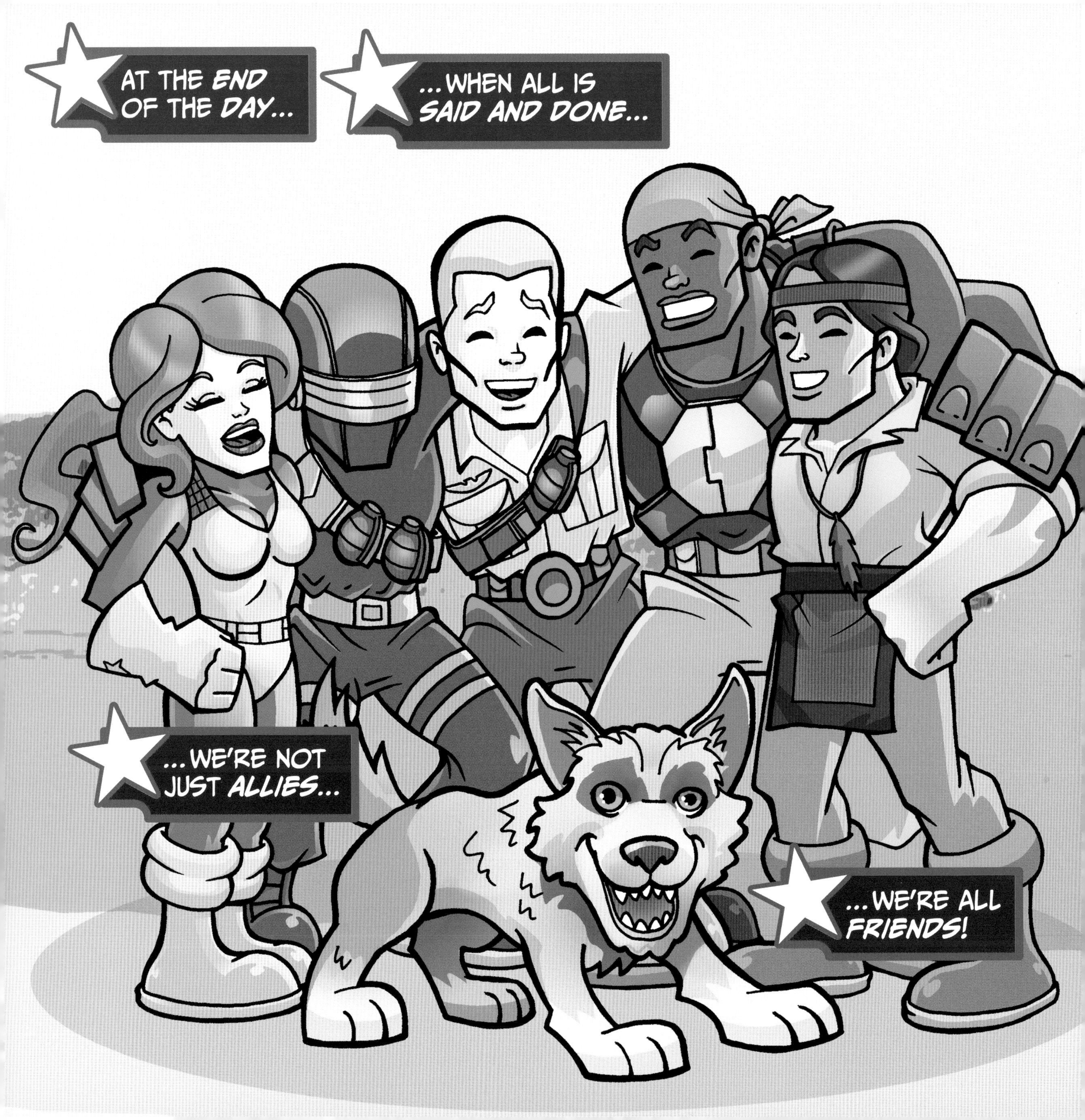

AT THE END OF THE DAY...
...WHEN ALL IS SAID AND DONE...
...WE'RE NOT JUST ALLIES...
...WE'RE ALL FRIENDS!

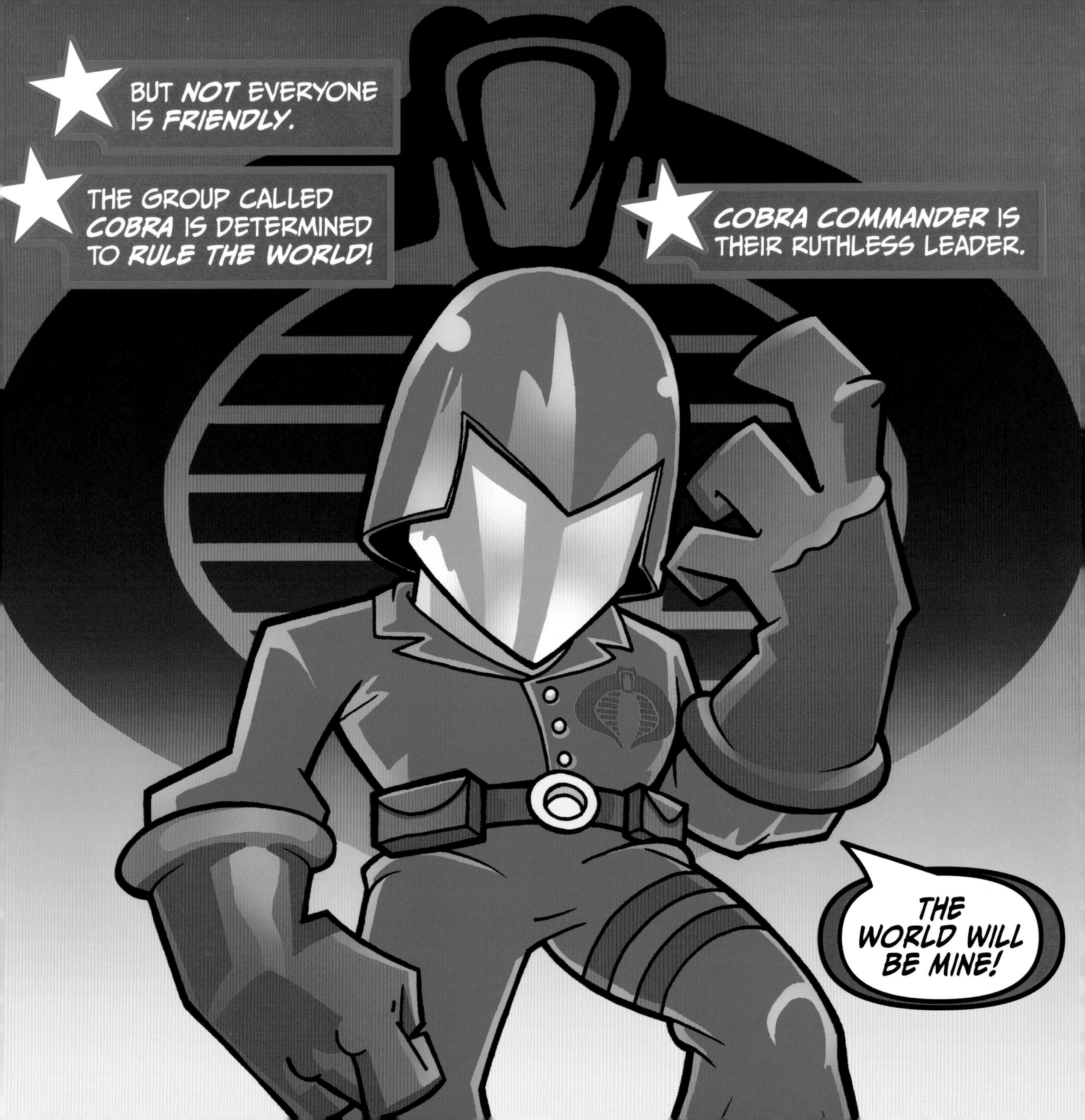
BUT NOT EVERYONE IS FRIENDLY.
THE GROUP CALLED COBRA IS DETERMINED TO RULE THE WORLD!
COBRA COMMANDER IS THEIR RUTHLESS LEADER.
THE WORLD WILL BE MINE!

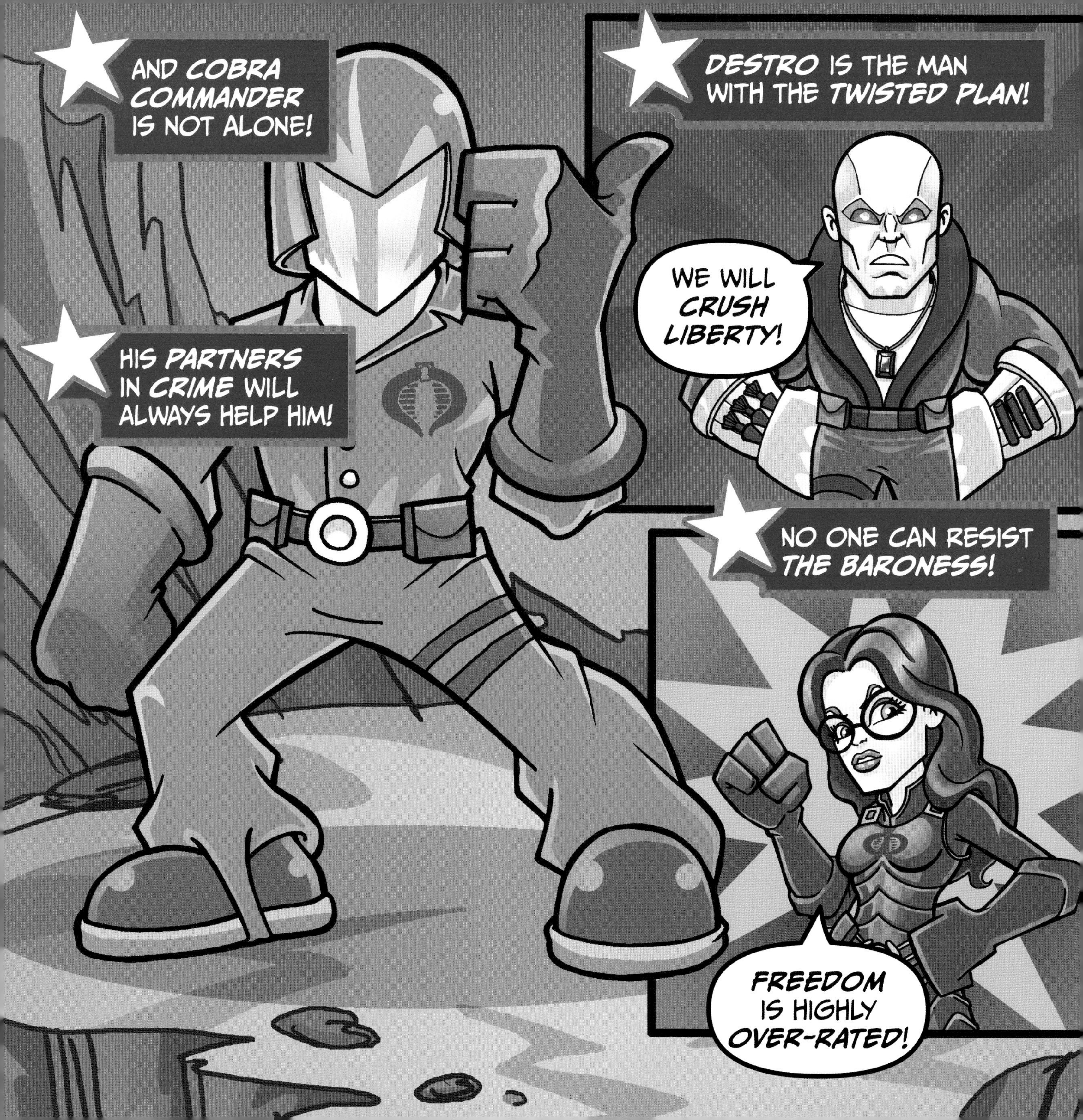
AND COBRA COMMANDER IS NOT ALONE!
HIS PARTNERS IN CRIME WILL ALWAYS HELP HIM!
DESTRO IS THE MAN WITH THE TWISTED PLAN!
WE WILL CRUSH LIBERTY!
NO ONE CAN RESIST THE BARONESS!
FREEDOM IS HIGHLY OVER-RATED!

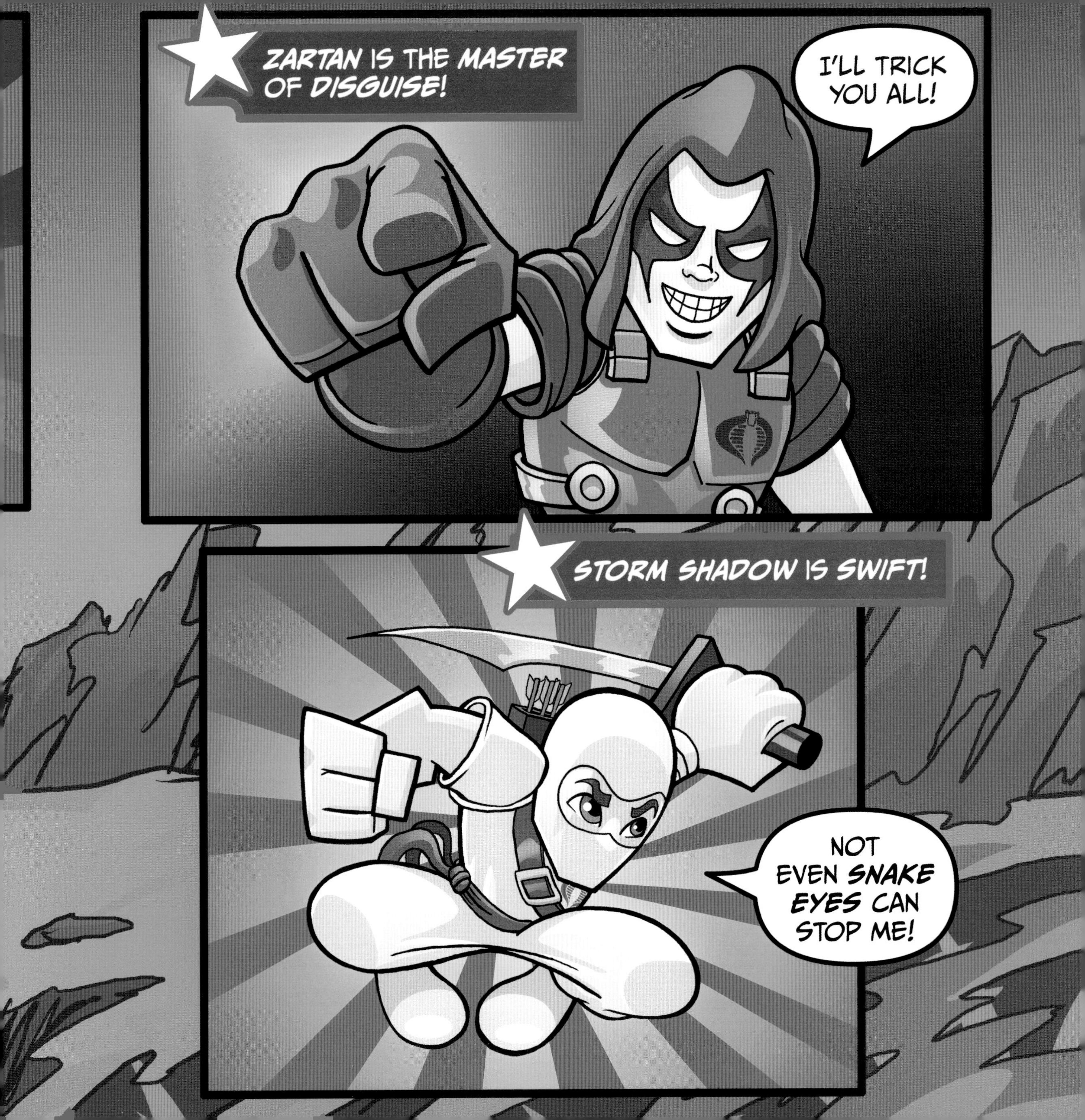

ZARTAN IS THE MASTER OF DISGUISE!
I'LL TRICK YOU ALL!
STORM SHADOW IS SWIFT!
NOT EVEN SNAKE EYES CAN STOP ME!

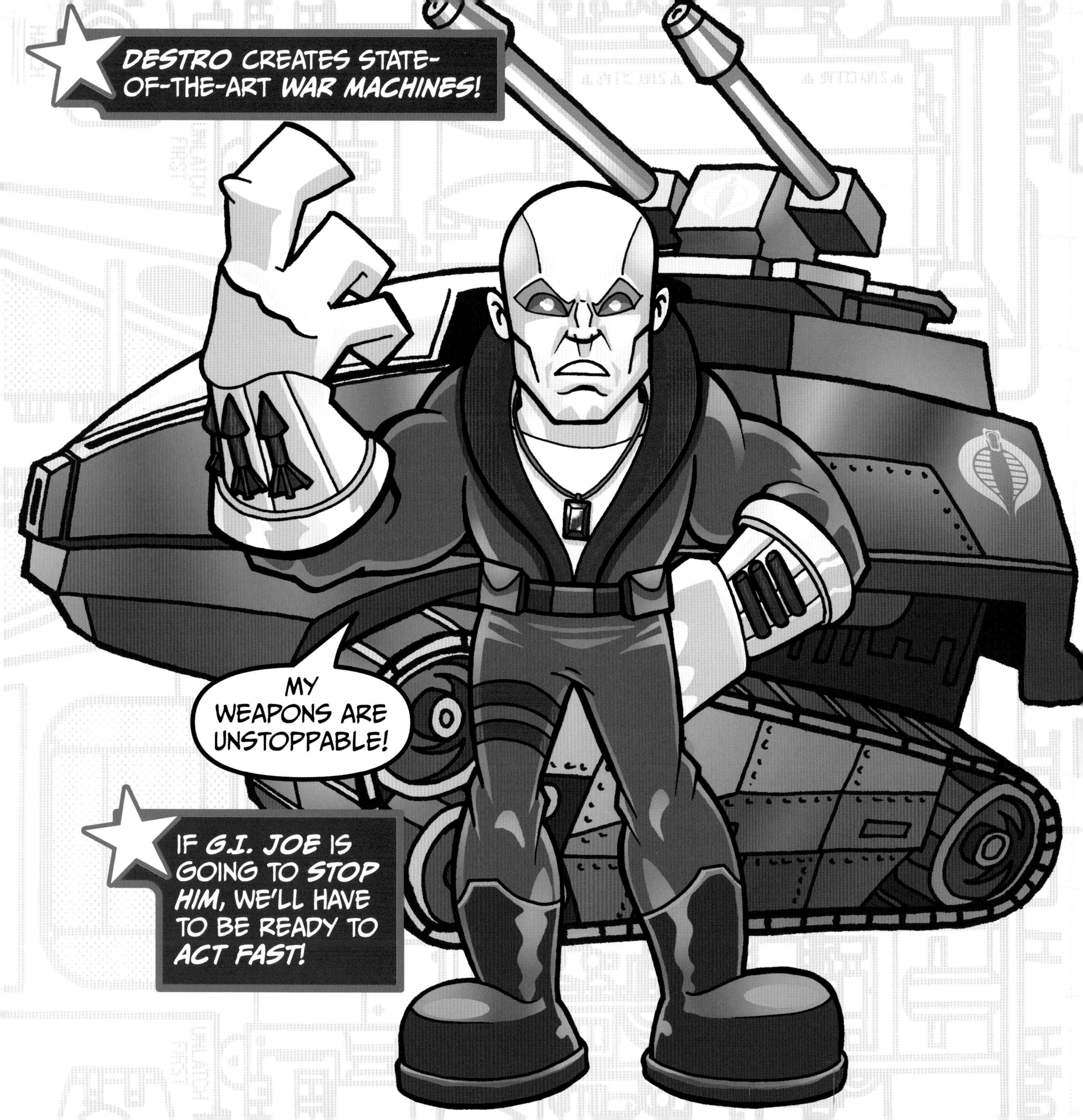
DESTRO CREATES STATE-OF-THE-ART WAR MACHINES!
MY WEAPONS ARE UNSTOPPABLE!
IF G.I. JOE IS GOING TO STOP HIM, WE'LL HAVE TO BE READY TO ACT FAST!

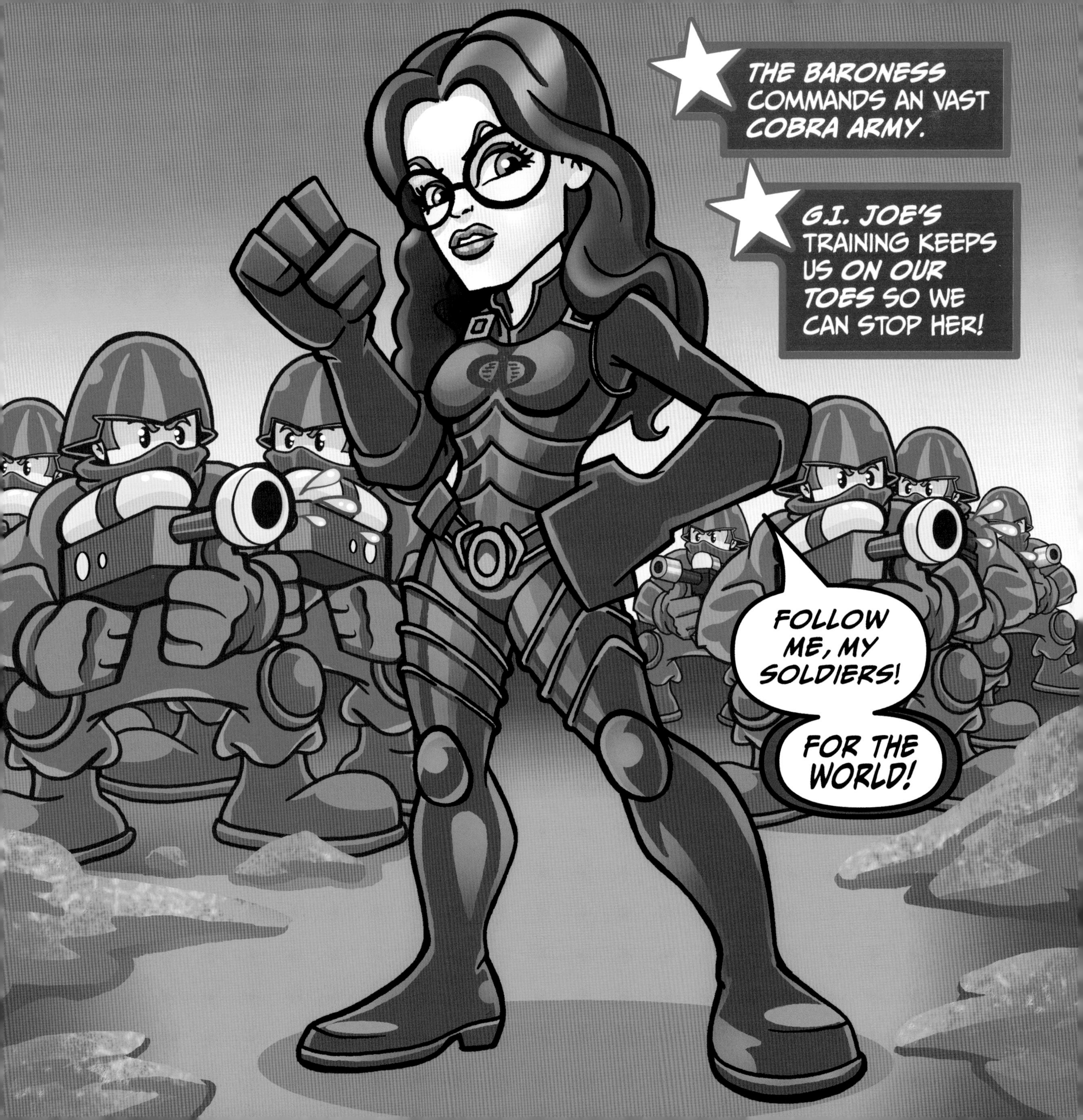
THE BARONESS COMMANDS AN VAST COBRA ARMY.
G.I. JOE'S TRAINING KEEPS US ON OUR TOES SO WE CAN STOP HER!
FOLLOW ME, MY SOLDIERS!
FOR THE WORLD!

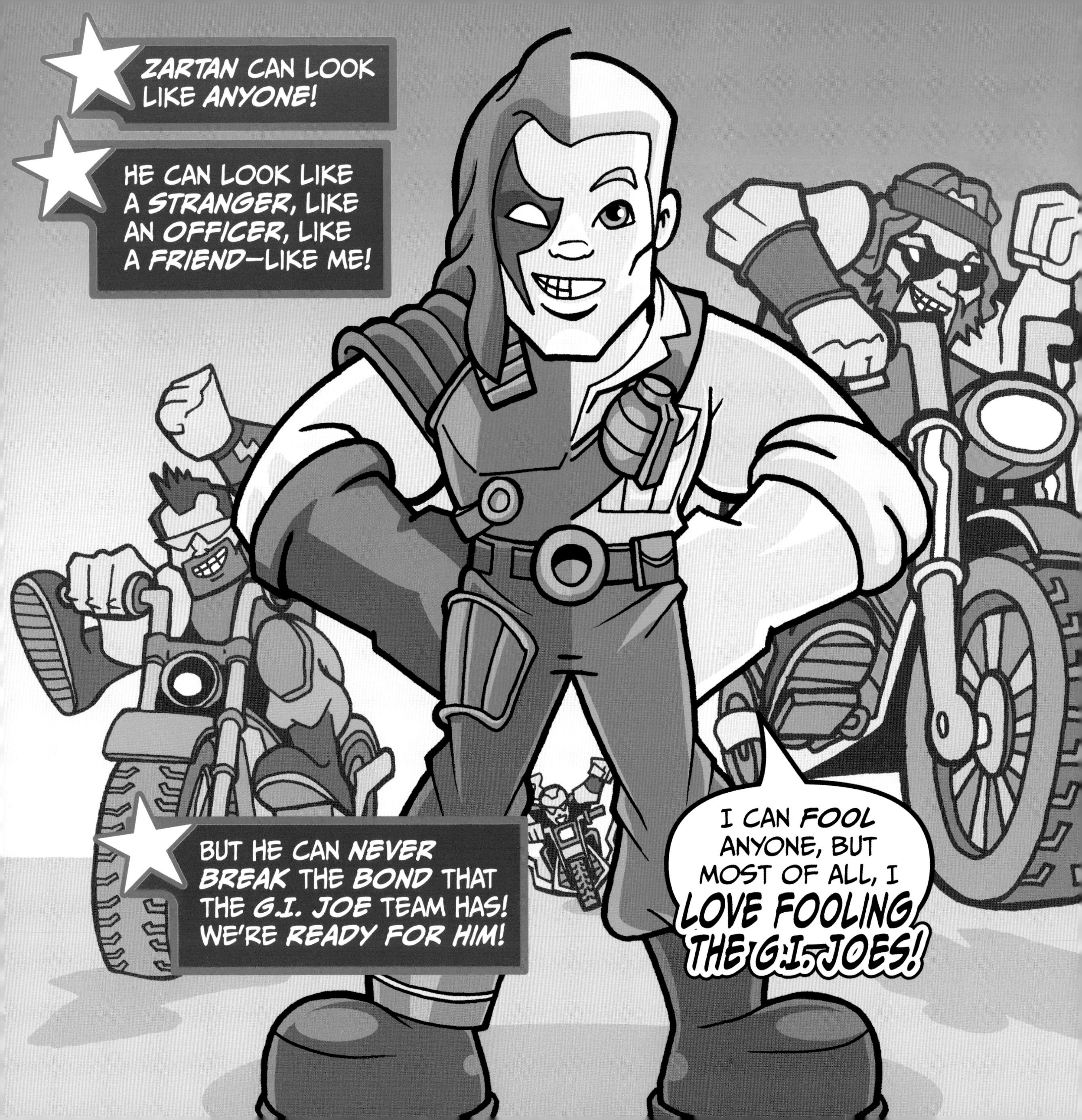
ZARTAN CAN LOOK LIKE ANYONE!
HE CAN LOOK LIKE A STRANGER, LIKE AN OFFICER, LIKE A FRIEND—LIKE ME!
BUT HE CAN NEVER BREAK THE BOND THAT THE G.I. JOE TEAM HAS! WE'RE READY FOR HIM!
I CAN FOOL ANYONE, BUT MOST OF ALL, I LOVE FOOLING THE G.I. JOES!

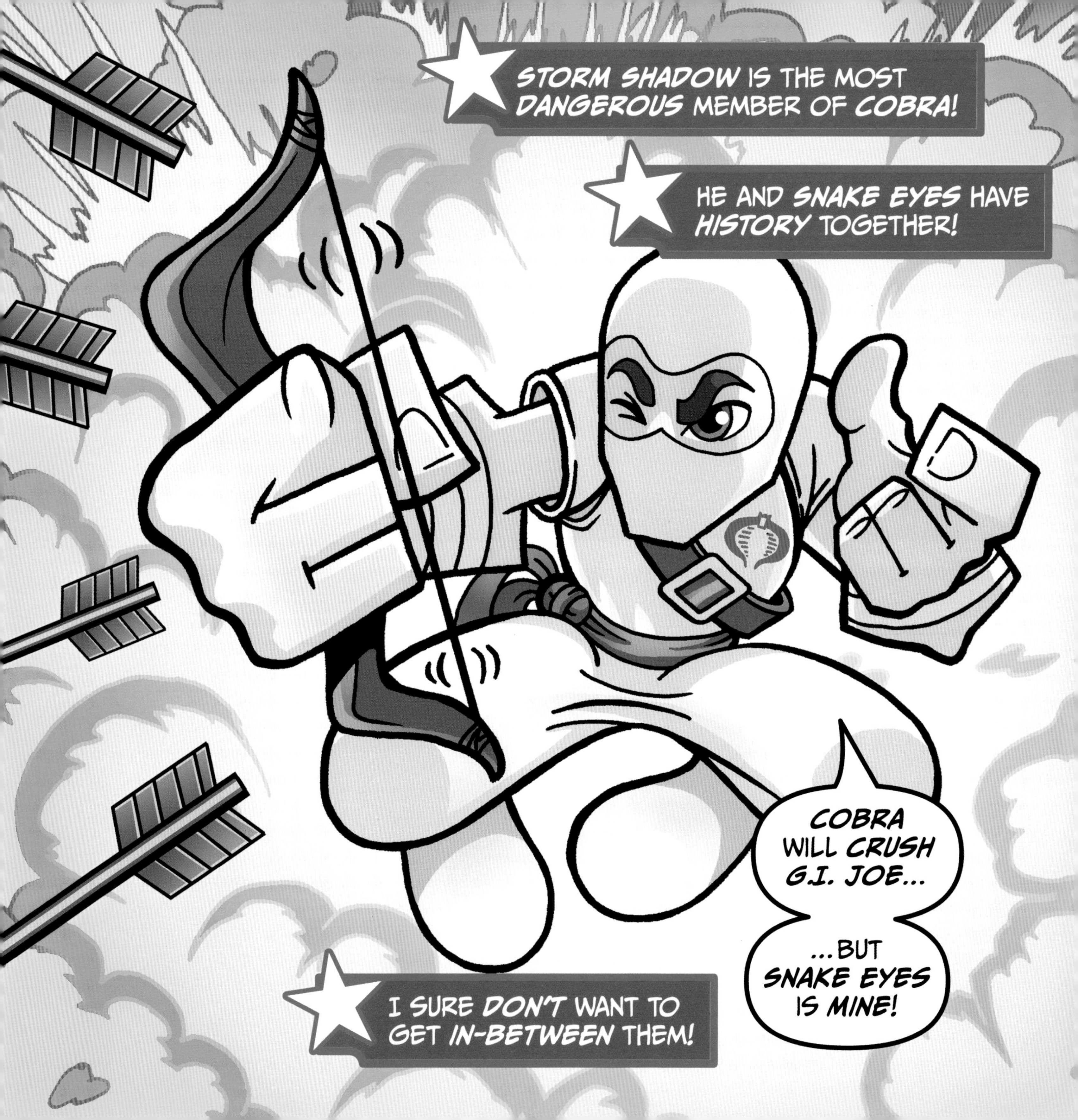
STORM SHADOW IS THE MOST DANGEROUS MEMBER OF COBRA!
HE AND SNAKE EYES HAVE HISTORY TOGETHER!
COBRA WILL CRUSH G.I. JOE...
...BUT SNAKE EYES IS MINE!
I SURE DON'T WANT TO GET IN-BETWEEN THEM!

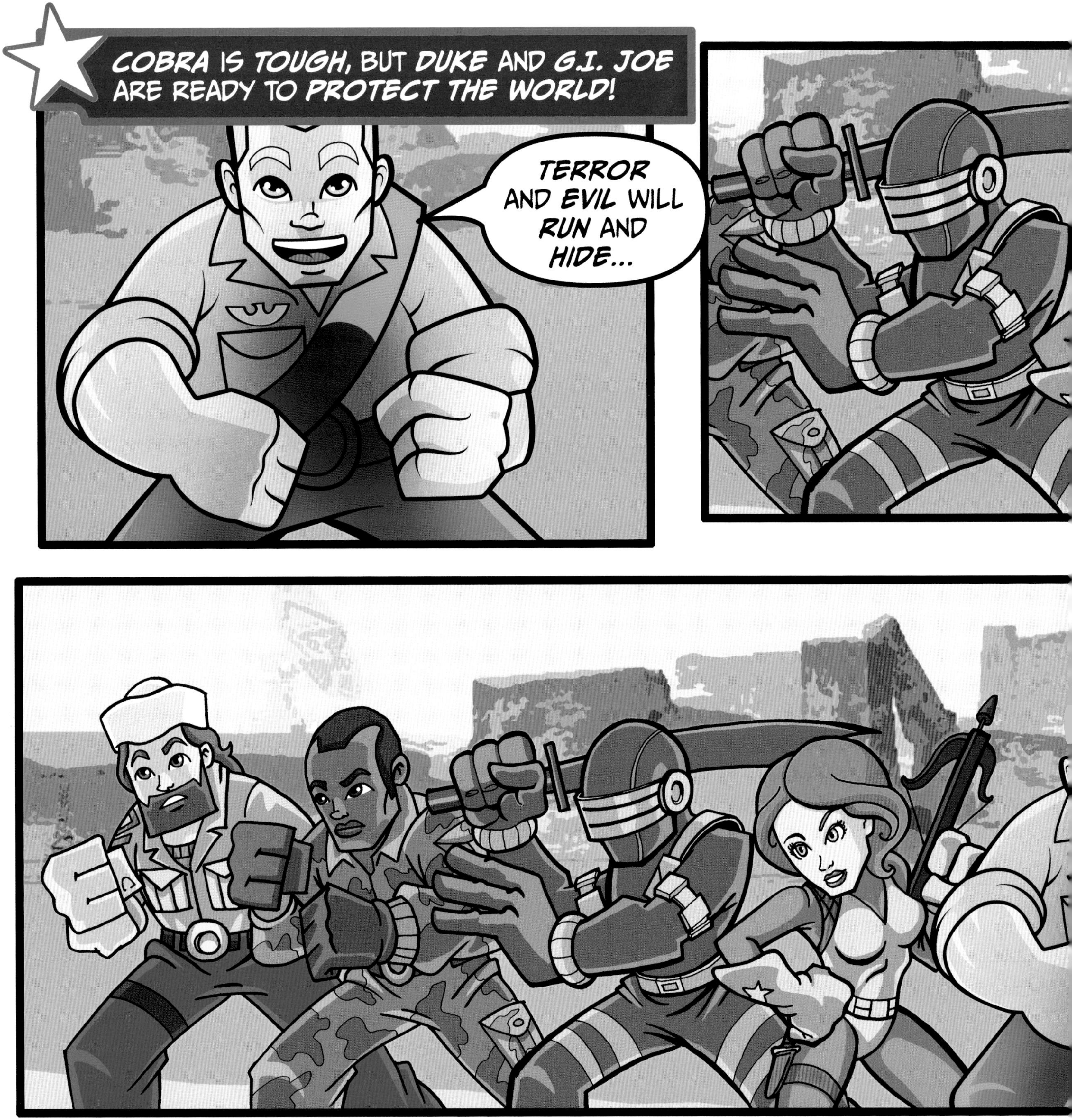
COBRA IS TOUGH, BUT DUKE AND G.I. JOE ARE READY TO PROTECT THE WORLD!
TERROR AND EVIL WILL RUN AND HIDE...

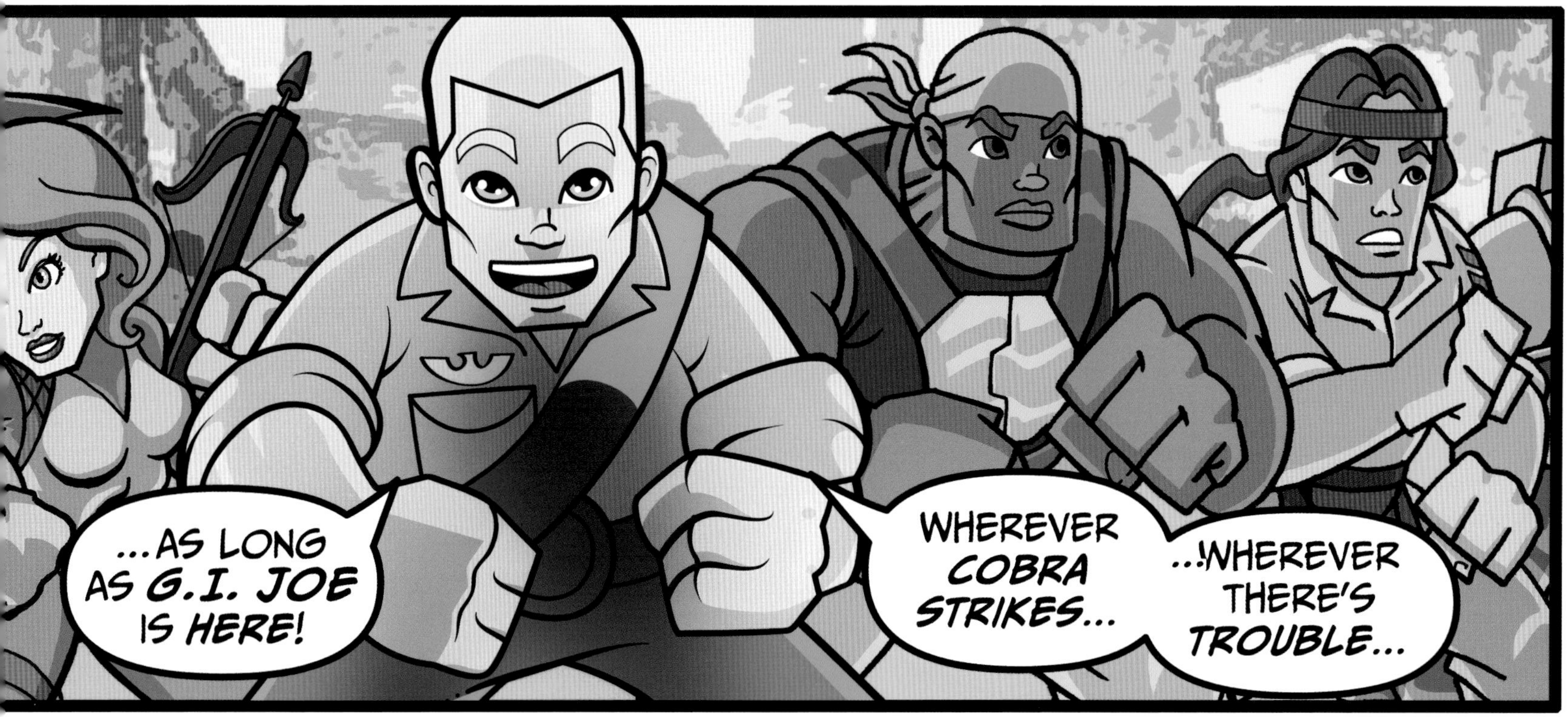
...AS LONG AS G.I. JOE IS HERE!
WHEREVER COBRA STRIKES...
...WHEREVER THERE'S TROUBLE...

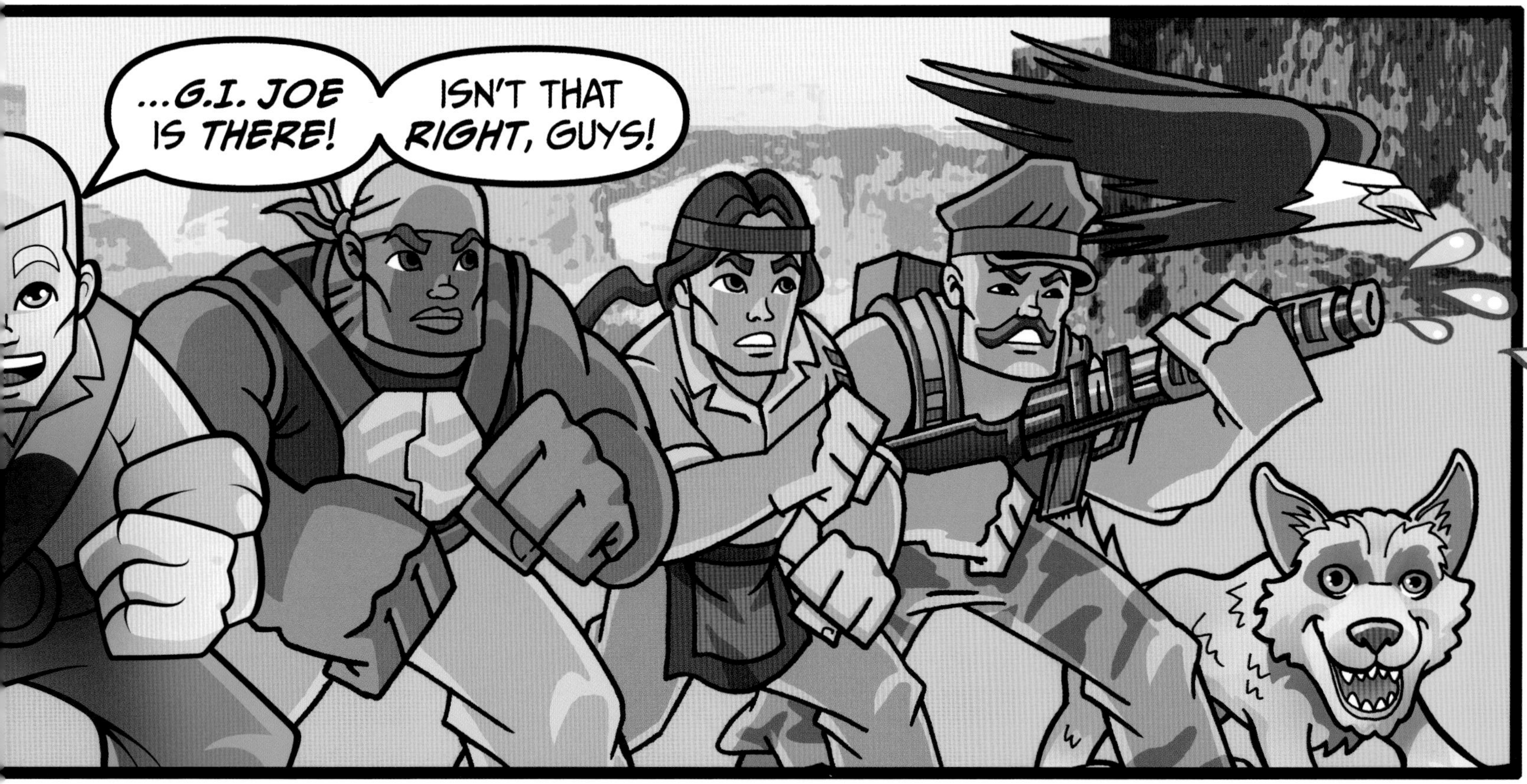
...G.I. JOE IS THERE!
ISN'T THAT RIGHT, GUYS!

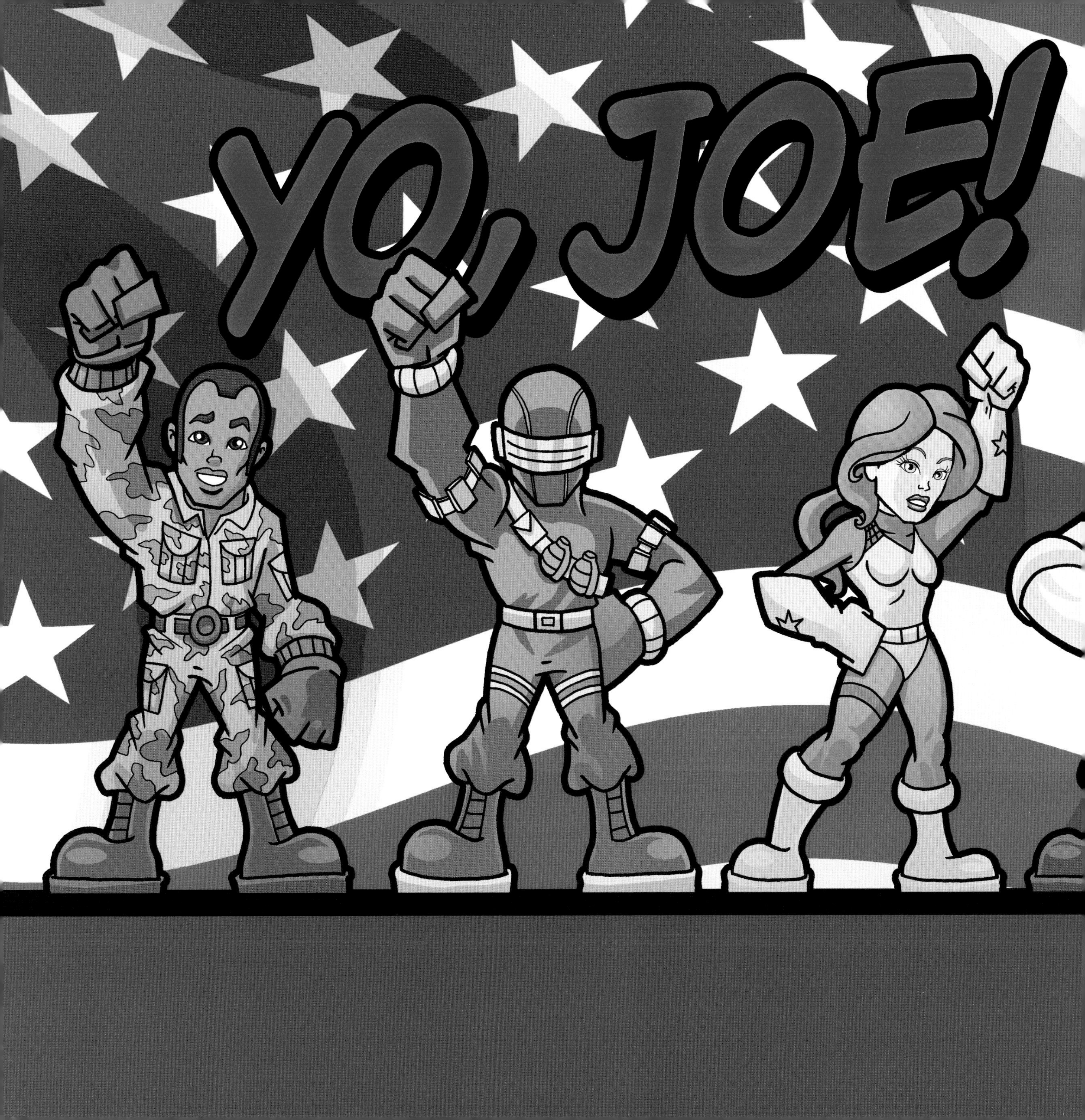
YO, JOE!

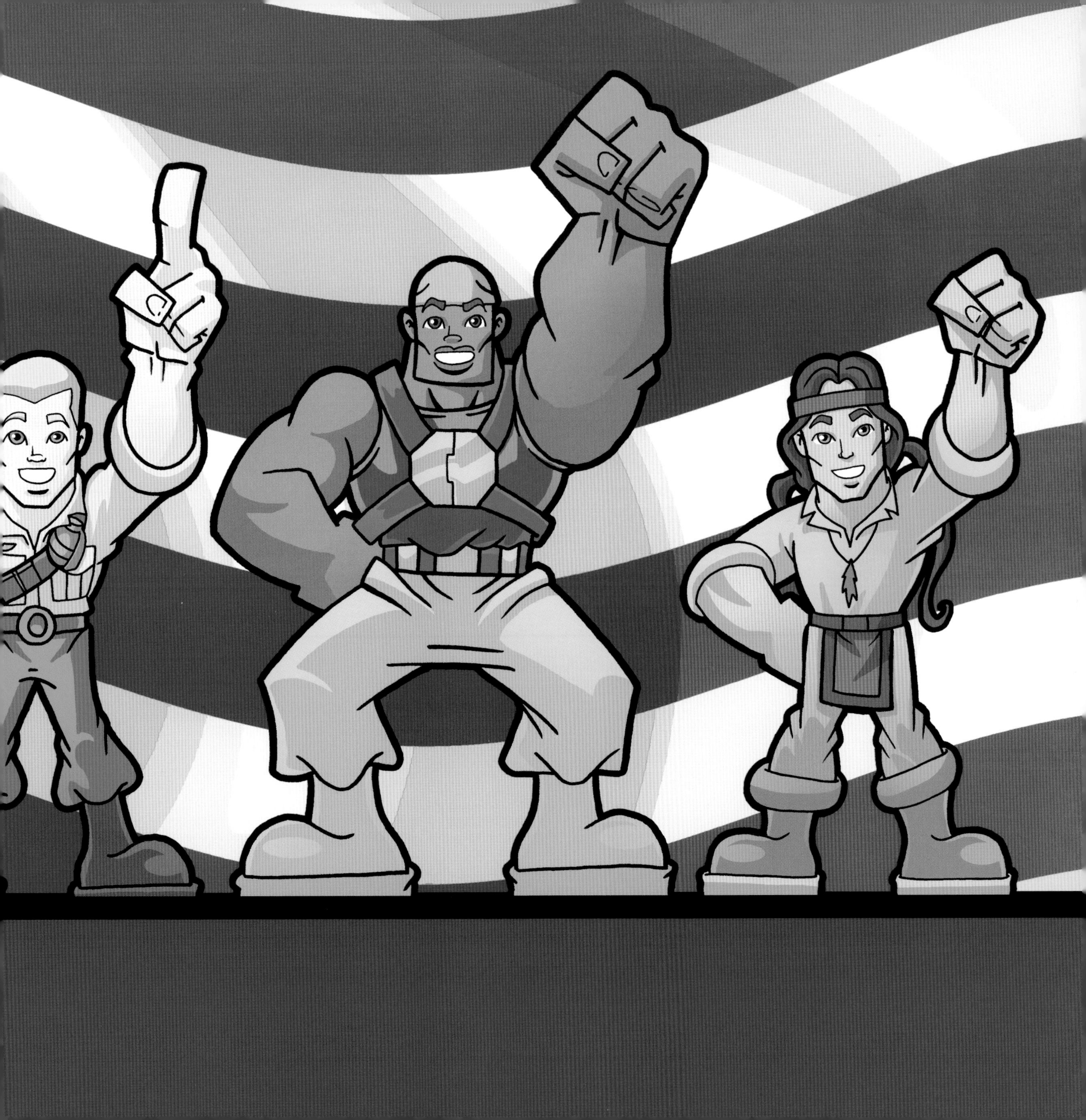

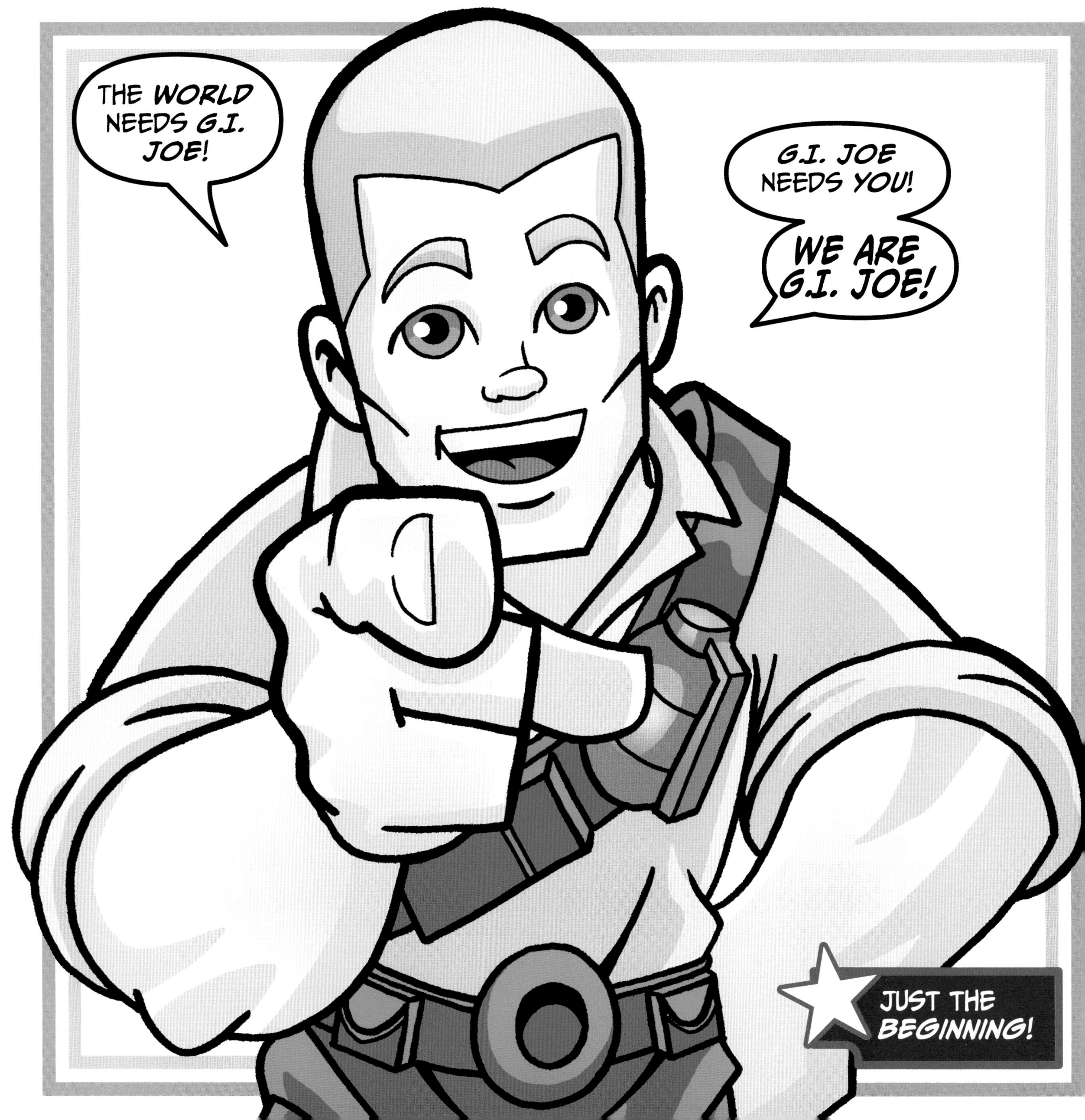
THE WORLD NEEDS G.I. JOE!
G.I. JOE NEEDS YOU!
WE ARE G.I. JOE!
JUST THE BEGINNING!